AUSTRALIA MODERN

STEVE HUYTON

15 HOUSES IN HARMONY WITH THE LAND

Foreword by
University of Adelaide
Professor Phil Harris

SCHIFFER PUBLISHING
4880 Lower Valley Road • Atglen, PA 19310

CONTENTS

FOREWORD FINDING OUR PLACE

Before the West arrived to stay in 1788, Australia was a fluid arrangement of nations, of people adapted to live sustainably in their lands. For the people of each nation, the land was them, and they were the land. Mythical ancestry gave names and stories to the land. Language flowered responsively, reinforcing boundaries as intermarriage reduced them. The land was sung, and the land sang back. This arrangement, this quilt of nations, had been in place for more than 50,000 years, a global record.

And, yes, in this context there was architecture—as diverse in its purpose and form as the nations and their particular environments and cultural ways. The architecture was very much about site selection and planning, about orientation for purpose and protection from the elements. Structures were created for refuge and to support being out there at the edge of comfort, looking out. Outdoor and transitional spaces were framed for social use. Fire was integrated, inside or out. Many were concerned with public and private and gender and age division. Always there was a seasonal usage. Materials were selected from what the place offered. By our Western measure, these crude assemblages of raw local resources were not seen as an architecture to learn from—they were too makeshift, too ephemeral. Mere camps.

Yet, on my reading, Australian architecture today is striving to take us back there. From the early 1970s we've been called to this by father figures of that time—Richard Leplastrier, Glenn Murcutt, Gabriel Poole. They reminded us to respond to site—topography, the local play of sun and wind, and the passage of seasons. And to build lean. Their acolytes are now established practitioners and in turn have shaped a next generation to carry the baton of environmental engagement, perhaps with even-greater verve.

This is quite a shift, since, in the almost 230 years postinvasion, we've built as the British homeland dictated, far more formally and solidly than the Aboriginal vernacular, and far more invariably with regard to site and place. First up, the Georgian box ruled in rudimentary shacks, in humble timber cottages, in masonry mansions and terraces; in towns, out bush; up north, down south, on the coast, in the Hills, in the desert. Boxes appeared as bastions in a hostile land. These were houses; anything else was a camp.

As Aboriginal population and land management declined, inversely, the scope for Georgian ostentation grew, heralding decoration as a semiotic appliqué. In time, verandas became essential additions, if not for climatic purposes or functional use, as gestures of having conquered the natural setting. But, lately, across our suburbs we see a reversion from this lighter, symbolic layer. The unlayered box seems to be back, and on steroids. Is it that we're less assured? Is it air conditioning? A life lived indoors on electronic devices? Globalism?

The shift led by our architectural father figures swims now against a new tide, which makes this book important. It also arises as Aboriginal people reassert themselves in this country.

And the shift flickers in Stephen Huyton's wide gathering of contemporary Australian houses, for they all tussle with the locales in which they are built. The flicker flares more strongly in some than others, but as we dig in to understand each project, we indeed find them to be environmentally aware creations. They are not houses by Leplastrier, Murcutt, or Poole, nor are many by their immediate followers. Rather, mostly they are by a scattering of younger Australian architects, illustrating the strength of direction imparted by our 1970s mentors.

Some projects are architecturally contextual, reflecting on what was solidly built locally before the current period. Others are freer inventions. All eschew the Georgian box and its recent revival. Some take us much closer to camping.

A few dwellings are small; others, multimillion-dollar extravagances. While particular houses are clearly memorable as objects, none are object centered in their instigation. Their forms, irrespective of scale, derive from a fit to topography and physical site contexts, and opportunity for solar orientation and prospect. There are skins that temper environmental connection, that might respond to season.

There is not much bling in this collection—decoration for decoration's sake. Rather, much use is made of natural materials, often in their raw state.

These houses are all one-offs, responding to particular people and places. Yet, the practice of architecture has always been in part a political action, so it is not surprising that inherent in the selected projects are leads for broader application—for example, in the brave use of raw and recycled materials, refined engineering, adaptable space, and energy-efficient design.

To me, as a body of work, these projects affirm a move to a connection with site and the great outdoors (that enduringly oft-touted host of the Australian lifestyle). This connection can be an unfolding through intermediary spaces or layers of operable building skins—but there is always a steadfast reaching out.

The represented architects pull solar passive design levers to create fitting designs both for temperate and tropical zones. It's probably a sad commentary on our modern fit to this continent, which skews to the southeastern coastal rim, that the so-called arid interior is not represented.

Reviewing the work, I see overall an expression of *longing to reduce*, to come to a *more indigenous* connection—rather than a celebration that we have already arrived at an "Australian" architecture.

Through the selected work we are shown diverse threads that might yet gather in a singular weave. For now they remain joyous individual celebrations of invention within a strong awareness of environmental context. Perhaps, though, in some instances, invention becomes a driver that drives too hard.

As you read on, 65,000 years after first settlement, I leave you with words that might act as an accompanying filter:

> *"The problem with 21st-century architecture is that it strives to be desperately interesting. Desperately interesting architecture will not last; it will not become timeless."*
>
> —Glenn Murcutt, 2014

Phil Harris is a director of Troppo Architects and a professor in the School of Architecture and the Built Environment, University of Adelaide. With practice cofounder Adrian Welke, Harris is the 2014 AIA Gold Medalist and 2010 Global Sustainable Architecture Award laureate.

SEABERG HOUSE

Melbourne, Victoria

1

Kerstin Thompson Architects

Compact and camp-like, this holiday house harks back to the modest, ramshackle dwellings that once populated the coast—before people began building beach houses that looked like their suburban homes. It has a looseness and material lightness that characterizes much of KTA's work.

Asked to design a house that could shrink for the empty-nester couple and expand when the family gathers, principal Kerstin Thompson came up with a cluster of buildings connected by a timber platform and pergolas. The main core contains two bedrooms and a kitchen/living area. The detached kids' pod is outfitted with bunks and spills out to the garden through big garage doors, and a second pod contains a studio/guest suite.

The house's multilevel layout follows the contours of the gently sloping site. A south-facing lower deck flows out to the lawn and beach—a dumping ground for surfboards, wet towels, and sandy feet. "Here in Victoria, on the bottom of Australia, a lot of our coast is south facing, but the best sun is on the north," Thompson says. "A big thing with beach houses is how to get views of the sea to the south but find a sunny outdoor space on the opposite end of the building." In this case the core is transparent enough that the owners can see through it to the sea. "That's another reason the floor drops away; even when you're on the north deck, you have the full impact of the view," she says.

If the design is all about the outdoors, its defining feature is the manipulation of natural light. Slatted and perforated window screens act as a template that casts changing patterns throughout the interiors. "It's not fancy but it's been carefully thought through," Thompson says.

"The fact that you go outside to get to those buildings makes you aware of the environment. It's a good way to connect people to the site and its changing conditions, but also to provide pockets of privacy and separate noisy kids from adults."

"Australians are fairly informal; they leave their doors open and let whomever in, and beach houses encapsulate that attitude and connection to the outside, hanging out on your front steps."

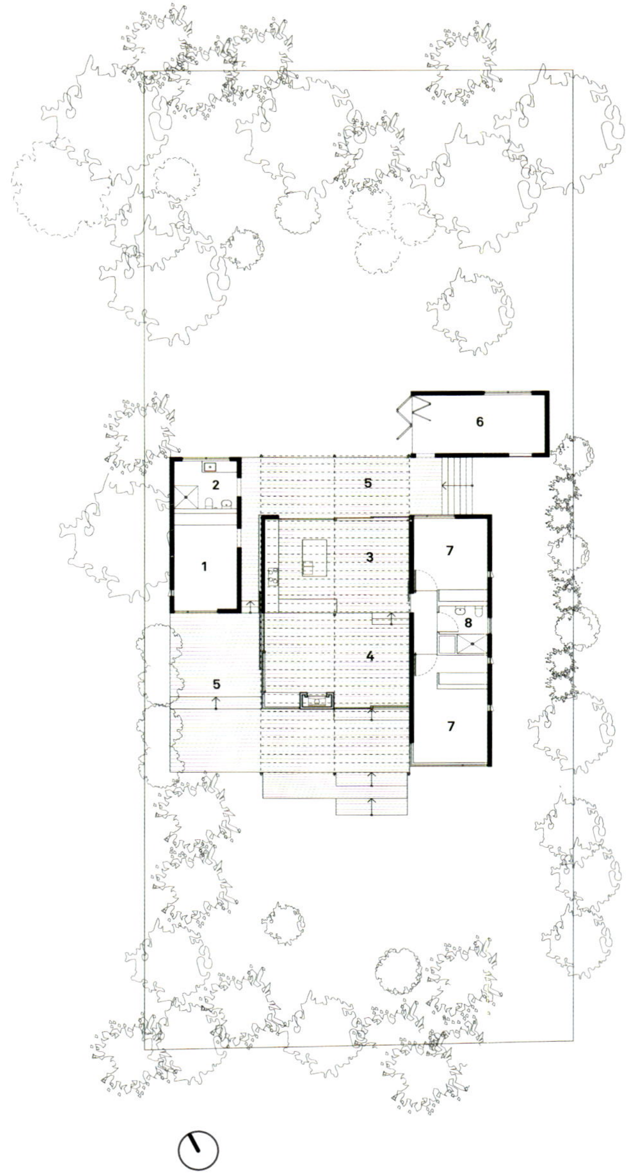

FLOOR PLAN

1 MASTER BEDROOM
2 MASTER BATH
3 DINING
4 LIVING
5 DECK
6 STUDIO
7 BEDROOM
8 BATHROOM

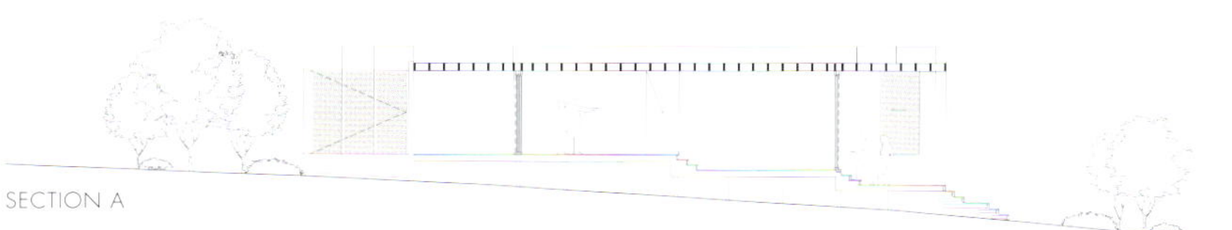
SECTION A

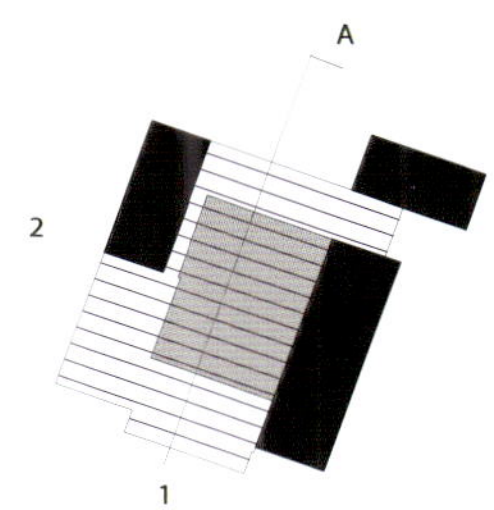
A
2
1

"The irony is that when you have architects doing low-key things, it feels quite gentle. This house is a lovely supporting background to different people's needs at different stages of life."

 Seaberg House, Kerstin Thompson Architects

❯ Spotted gum panels add richness, warmth, and intimacy to the bedroom walls and the floor of the core building. The darker color amplifies the landscape colors, and the indigenous hardwood has an appealing softness that is more durable than painted plasterboard.

⌄ KTA likes to use materials that don't require a finish. The exterior's compressed cement sheets are durable and recall the cladding of old beach shacks. Because it's a sheet product, it is visually lighter than a masonry wall. The panels, which also form the interior walls, are perforated on the east and west to form sun shades, and small flaps allow for ventilation.

 Seaberg House, Kerstin Thompson Architects

35a

SKY BARN

Adelaide, South Australia

2

Max Pritchard Architect

In designing a home in an inner suburb of Adelaide, architect Max Pritchard used a number of time-tested strategies to help regulate indoor temperatures while creating a piece of art. Conceived as three pavilions set in a pool courtyard, the north-facing, two-story main volume puts the kitchen, dining, and lounge areas on the upper level, with the garage and utility rooms below. This elevated position allows the living spaces to capture winter sun and a distant view of the hills—which, under normal circumstances, is almost impossible in a neighborhood of tightly spaced lots. The black polished-concrete floor acts as a heat sink in winter, storing and slowly releasing the sun's energy, while roof overhangs shield the interior from the high summer sun.

The two rear pavilions—one houses the master suite across the pool, the other behind it contains two guest bedrooms—sit at a higher elevation than the front pavilion, following the land's natural slope from the street. Each pavilion is one room wide; "the advantage of pavilions is that they are narrow and can be naturally ventilated from either side," Pritchard says.

In addition to stairs, ramps make a unexpected appearance, linking the levels and pavilions. "The owners are devoted to their little dachshunds, and the dogs can't go up staircases," Pritchard says. "It's also a nice way of journeying from one pavilion to another and allows older people to access the living area. A lot of houses I do these days have a lift alternative, but this is nice."

Despite its simplicity, marine plywood, made from economical hoop pine native to Australia, is used to dramatic effect. It wraps the garage door, the pivoting entry door, and the main living space's cathedralized ceiling. The plywood and stone are a glowing counterpoint to the black-and-white interiors and dark exterior surfaces. At night, this finely detailed house is like a quiet lantern on the street, illuminating the landscape without calling attention to itself.

› The countertop pierces the glass wall to anchor an outdoor kitchen.

›› Pritchard covered the main pavilion's lower concrete block volume in smooth stucco, while the second story and roof are clad in metal sheeting that folds into fins on the south side. Glass louvers provide ventilation and light.

One of the resident dachshunds demonstrates the alternative route for short legs. The ramps between levels and pavilions also future-proof the house both for owners and guests and offer a more interesting journey than an enclosed elevator.

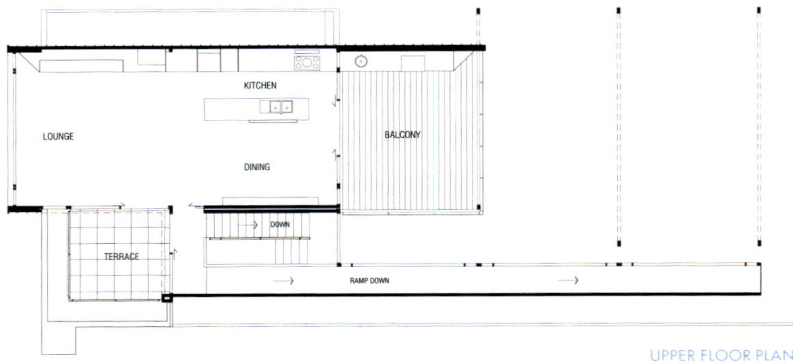

UPPER FLOOR PLAN

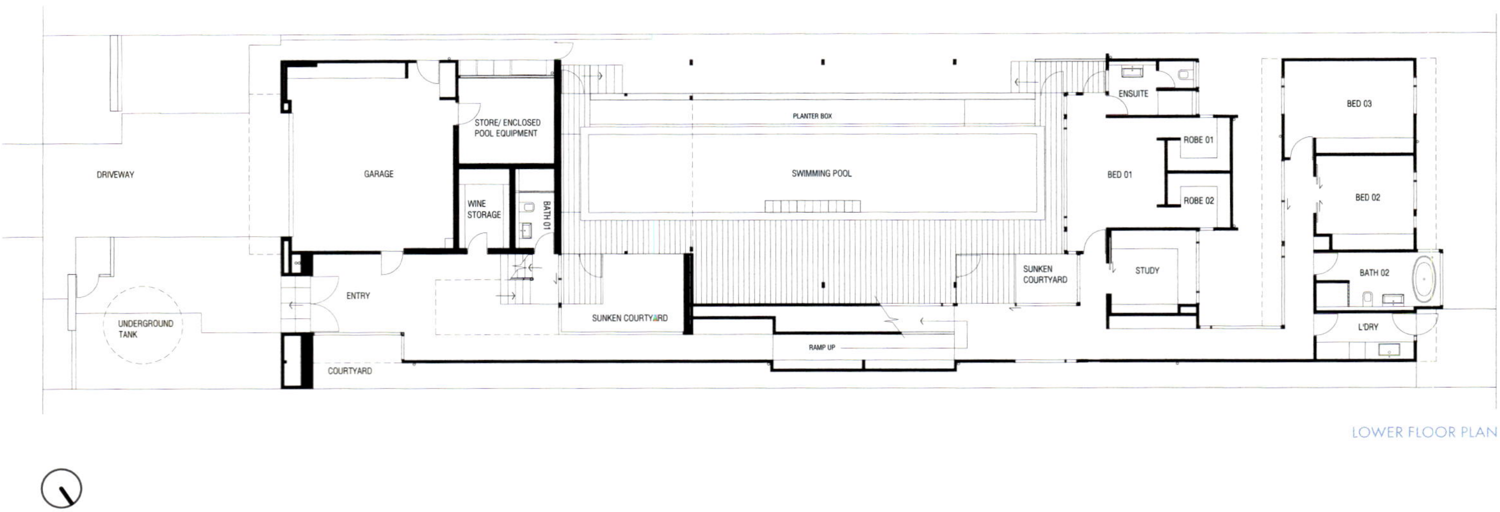

LOWER FLOOR PLAN

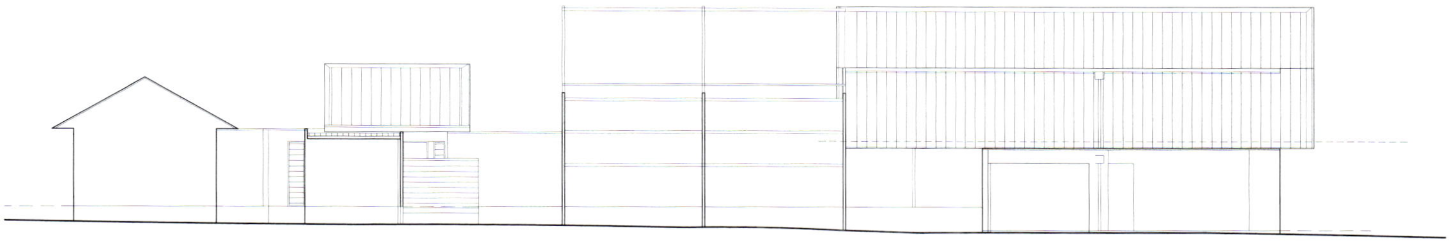

SOUTHWEST ELEVATION

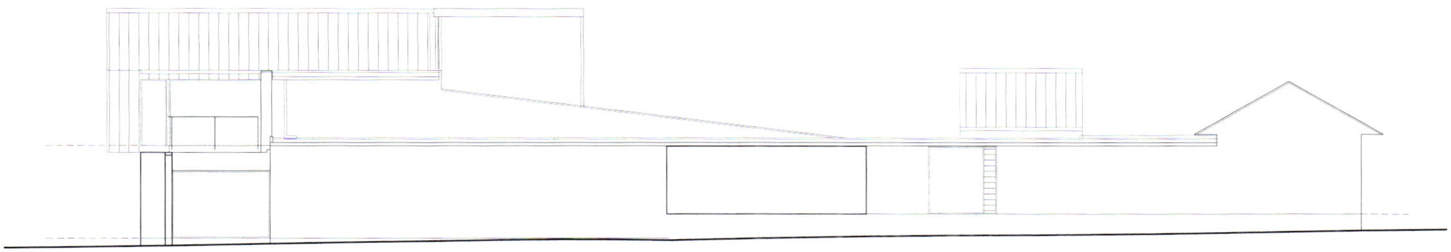

NORTHEAST ELEVATION

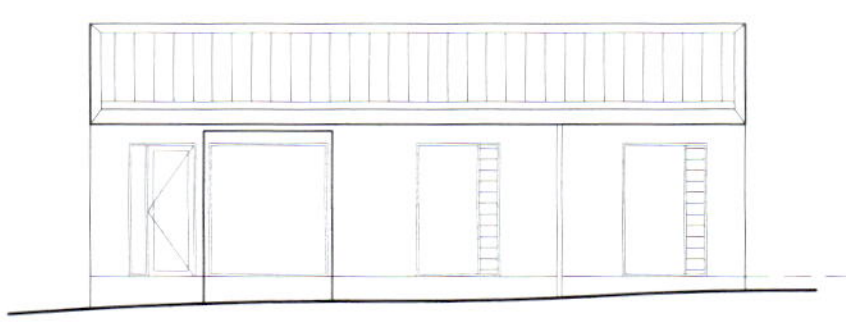

NORTHWEST ELEVATION

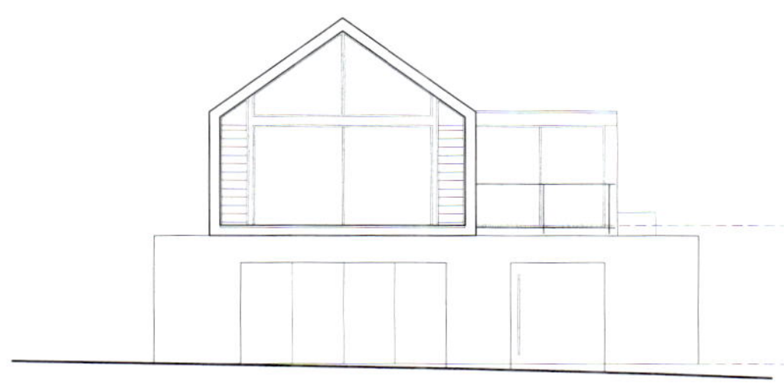

SOUTHEAST ELEVATION

«« The master bedroom sits on axis with the lap pool, inviting the owners, who are avid swimmers, to take a daily morning dip. Its high steel frame has motorized fabric shades that roll down into a box. A tallowwood screen and pool deck create a tranquil oasis that recalls Japanese courtyards.

^ A thickly vegetated courtyard separates the master suite and rear guest pavilion.

TOY MANAGEMENT HOUSE

Melbourne, Victoria

3

Austin Maynard Architects

This complex house is full of ideas, but they revolve around two core elements: the use of white perforated metal to sift sunlight into dark spaces and shield areas overpowered by sunlight, and flooring that swallows up children's toys while keeping them within easy reach.

Located on a tight semiurban lot, the row house packs a lot of light, air, and living into its roughly 6-meter (20-foot) width. After removing the back of the one-story house, Austin Maynard Architects replaced it with a two-story volume containing two bedrooms and a bath. A planted courtyard between the old and new sections acts as a large light well that brings a view of the sky into the center of the house. That light reaches the second story through white perforated steel on the staircase and upstairs hallway floor, which allows sunlight from large second-story windows to filter down to the living areas too.

Downstairs, the floor plan follows a playful logic, its pieces falling unexpectedly into place like a giant, three-dimensional puzzle. Wood flooring unites the bedroom, study, bath, and entry corridor in the original part of the house. A brick floor takes over at the kitchen and continues through the house into the backyard. Just past the kitchen, one steps up onto a plywood platform that serves both as a floor and a giant storage box with hinged cubbies for camping gear (under the dining area) and children's toys (in the living area). As the architects described it, "The endless management of stuff was the key. Gravity is colluding with your child and conspires in its favor. Parents constantly pick things up, while kids throw them down."

At 45 centimeters high (17.5 inches), the platform wraps around the central seating area, creating a conversation pit and ad hoc seating ledge. "You can see the brick floor in that area, so that no matter where you are, you understand that the brick floor is flowing right through the house and someone has plopped on this semipermanent elevated platform," says principal Mark Austin. With this built-in flexibility, the owners can take away the wood cubbies as their needs change.

The interior's white perforated metal panels reappear along the northwest-facing rear facade, which gets the most aggressive sunlight of the day. They are set a few feet out from the foldaway glass wall to create a shaded indoor-outdoor space, and the lacy shield seems to shift from opaque to translucent depending on the light and time of day.

Other features also help conserve natural resources. A white roof reduces heat buildup, solar panels supply off-the-grid electricity, and a water tank buried in the courtyard captures roof water used to flush toilets and water the garden.

"We made gravity the parents' ally by making the floor one big toy box. Let's get a broom and sweep all the Legos in."

› Sliding wall panels on the upstairs master bedroom can be closed for privacy or opened to the airy corridor, expanding the bedroom by almost 2 meters (6.5 feet).

"We like to open houses so you can have conversations across a light well or floor to floor. You have visual and acoustical connections, but also the ability to hide yourself away with sliding doors."

› A seamless, custom fiberglass tub eliminates places where grime and mold can gather, while a slim gutter along the walls funnels splashed water to a floor drain.

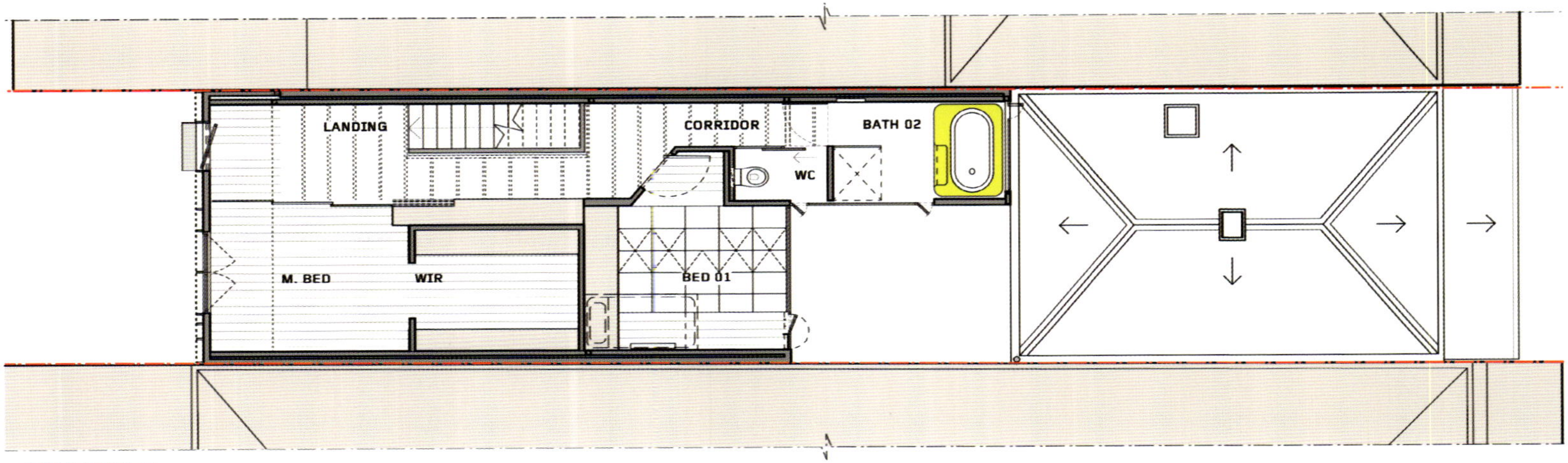

FIRST FLOOR PLAN

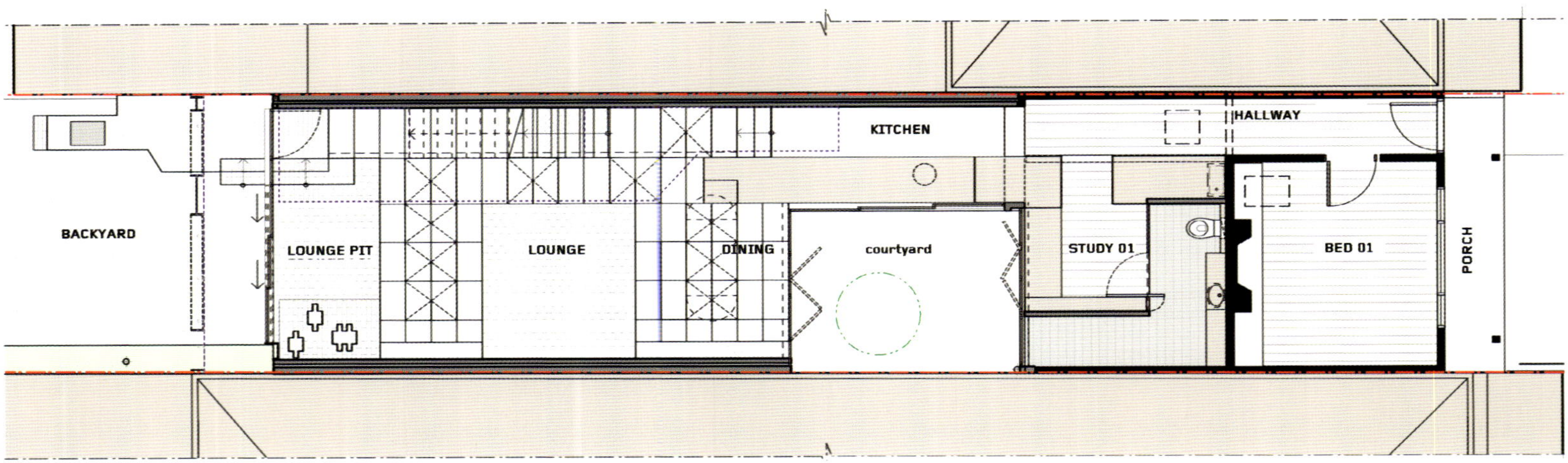

GROUND FLOOR PLAN

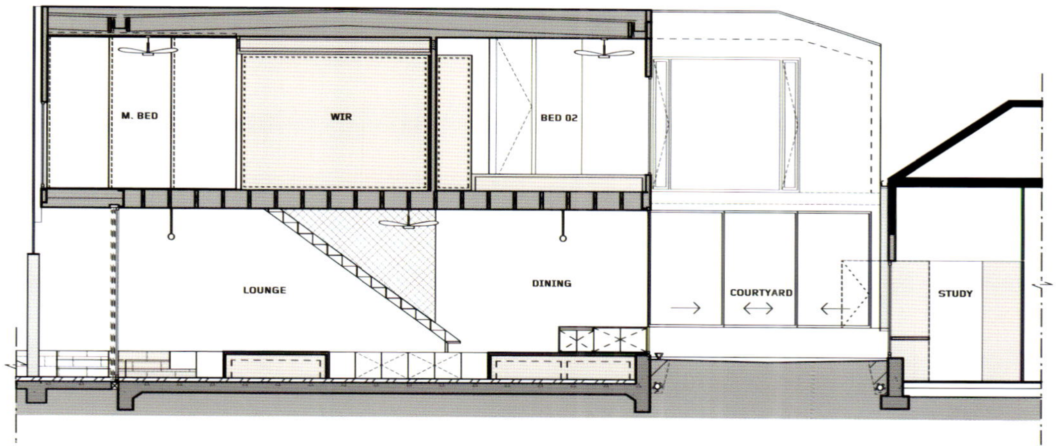

LONG SECTION

The perforated metal facade feels solid and protective on a bright, hot day. When the sun fades, the facade appears translucent and the metal skin feels more like lace than a wall.

NARANGA HOUSE

Gold Coast, Queensland

4

James Russell Architect

Architect James Russell describes this diaphanous house as a village square. It is transparent enough to invite interaction both with the local climate and other people—on the street and inside the house, from room to room and floor to floor. Located in Florida Gardens, a canal neighborhood dating to the 1950s, the building envelope's multiple layers provide varying degrees of privacy and climate control. White extruded bricks, laid on their sides to show the holes and affixed to timber studs, form a continuous screen around the house. The interior-facing layer varies between textured glass and opaque fiber-cement panels—a traditional material used on simple beach houses. In other sections, sliding glass doors are stepped in 30 centimeters (almost a foot) for easy cleaning and protection from the rain, and to create miniverandas.

The front door leads into a garden courtyard—"a hole from earth to sky"—where sliding glass walls allow the kitchen, living, and dining areas to be open to the breezes or closed off. Upstairs, four bedrooms and a sitting area lie along a corridor that looks into the sunlit courtyard below.

The house illustrates Russell's climate-driven design philosophy. A weatherproof curtain can be drawn across the southwest-facing back wall to shield against stormy weather and winter's chilly breezes. "It's a fairly idyllic climate where you need to manage certain conditions," says Russell. "Amazing summer storms come from the southwest. If you close down the southwest and open up to the northeast when storms are going over, you can really celebrate and be part of those storms."

Finely detailed but approaching a campsite's utilitarian logic, this house is an interesting set of contradictions. The costs of its complex detailing were offset by the use of self-finishing, off-the-shelf materials. Room dimensions were adjusted to work with stock materials, including kid-friendly melamine walls and ceilings and aluminum-frame glass doors.

The inexpensive patterned brick adds a touch of mid-twentieth-century Gold Coast glamour, a modern riff on the area's old breezeblock houses. While the owners initially wanted to use concrete breezeblock, it is prohibitively expensive now and has to be painted to be stable, Russell says. Made locally of clay, these extruded bricks are more efficient to produce than solid pressed bricks.

"The clay is squeezed through a machine to make a long line of clay that has holes in it, so it dries quickly and evenly in a kiln, and then is cut into brick-size pieces," Russell says. "You don't see the holes when they are laid normally, but the holes make a fine filigree or screen, which is what we were keen to get. It's like looking through the fine timber screens they used around upper levels of Moorish buildings that women occupied. It allows you to be veiled from almost anywhere in the house, but you can see back through the screen and are aware of what's going on across backyards or out on the street."

The house does a lot with a little, playing with notions of enclosure and exposure behind its inscrutable facade.

 Naranga House, James Russell Architect

The entry courtyard containing a crepe myrtle tree establishes a visual and acoustical connection between floors and brings the daylong northern sun into every part of the house.

"I hate the idea of a front door. It sets up a barrier between inside and outside, whereas arrival to this place is very much about the gate providing protection or security to a space that's both inside and outside."

‹ The absence of track work in the concrete floor slab minimizes the presence of pocketing doors that enclose the living and dining space.

FIRST FLOOR PLAN

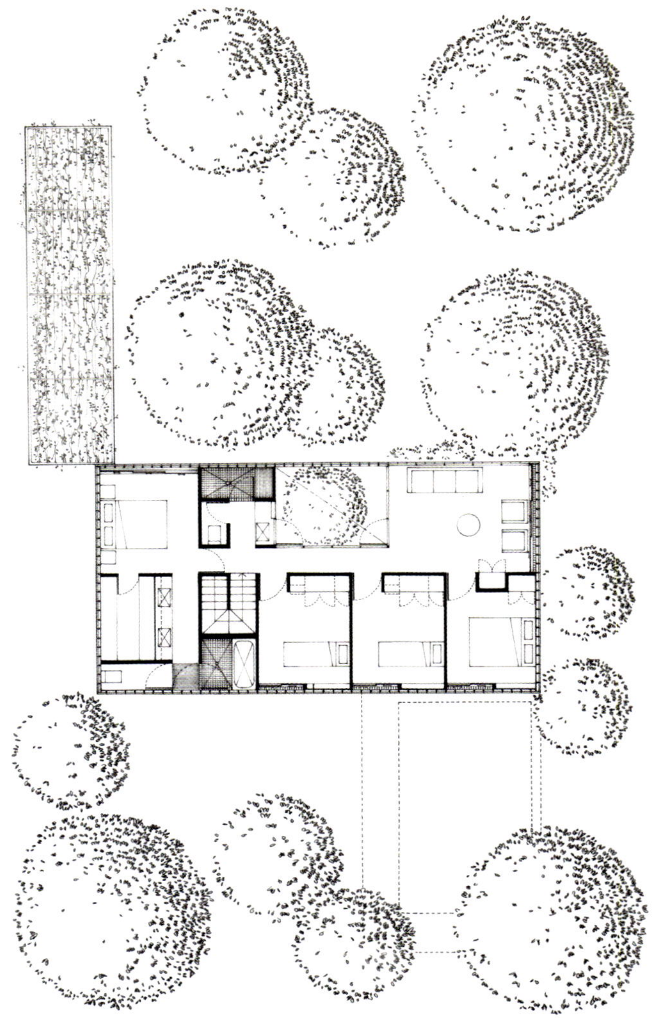

SECOND FLOOR PLAN

"I generally avoid applying any finish—the materials are just what they are—so the exterior is just a clay brick with a beautiful creamy color, not too intensely bright. Over time, a bit of dirt on it is fine, so it will age well. Another nice thing is that it's modeled on a Roman brick, so it is skinnier than other bricks, 40 millimeters [1.58 inches] high and 290 millimeters [11.42 inches] long," and it matches up with the standard framing dimensions behind it as it wraps around the building.

QUORROBOLONG HOUSE

Hunter Valley, New South Wales

Fergus Scott Architects

5

Streamlined and elegant, Quorrobolong House heeds the Aboriginal proverb to "touch the earth lightly." Roughly resembling an aircraft in plan, its two perpendicular wings hover off the ground on minimal pylons. The innovative structure addresses the possibility of ground-surface shifts as a result of longwall mining activity, an ongoing issue in parts of Australia, where Crown rights means that landowners don't own the minerals and petroleum beneath the surface.

Situated on a working cattle and olive farm, the house's wings pivot off a central kitchen/dining area—the only part of the building touching the ground. This communal space opens to a sunny courtyard to the north and a lawn to the south. The east wing contains the living room and master suite; the longer west wing, canted to capture southern views across the valley to the mountains, houses three bedrooms and two baths. A smaller building on the edge of the northern courtyard serves as a mudroom and privacy wall.

"We wanted a long building open to northern sun, but its length meant it had to be adjustable," says architect Fergus Scott. "The longer the house, the higher the possibility that it could be disturbed by uneven settlements in the ground caused by mining."

Structurally, the bedroom wings are designed as a "line of matchboxes" between parallel precast-concrete beams spanning up to 10 meters (32.8 feet), with steel portal frames sitting between the beams and supporting the timber floor structure, wall framing, and light galvanized-steel roof. In the event of ground-surface shifts, each wing can be cranked up or down with the use of flat jacks and steel shims inserted at the top of each pylon. Lapped roof sheets and hidden slip joints in the floor and ceiling allow the wings to move in sync with any future elevation adjustments.

The house lives lightly in a figurative way, too. A concrete floor in the central area soaks up heat from the low winter sun and releases it slowly during the day, and zoned heating and cooling allows parts of the house to be closed off when not in use. Doors and windows contain recycled hardwood, and the wings' flooring is made out of recycled local sweetgum trees. Being a country property, the house is also water independent. It collects and treats its own wastewater before dispersing it into the ground, and drinking water is captured from the roof. A 15-kilowatt solar array augments the house's power.

Scott has a flair not just for the functional but also for tone and texture. The exterior's gray concrete and warm, reddish-brown jarrah wood echo the trunk colors of spotted gum and ironbark trees on the grounds; from certain angles, it almost disappears into the bush.

> View of the house from the smaller utility building on the northern edge of the courtyard.

The glassy living spaces are one room wide, allowing light to wash through. The smaller building (visible through the window) acts as a privacy wall and contains wood-clad alcoves with washing facilities and storage for the farmworkers.

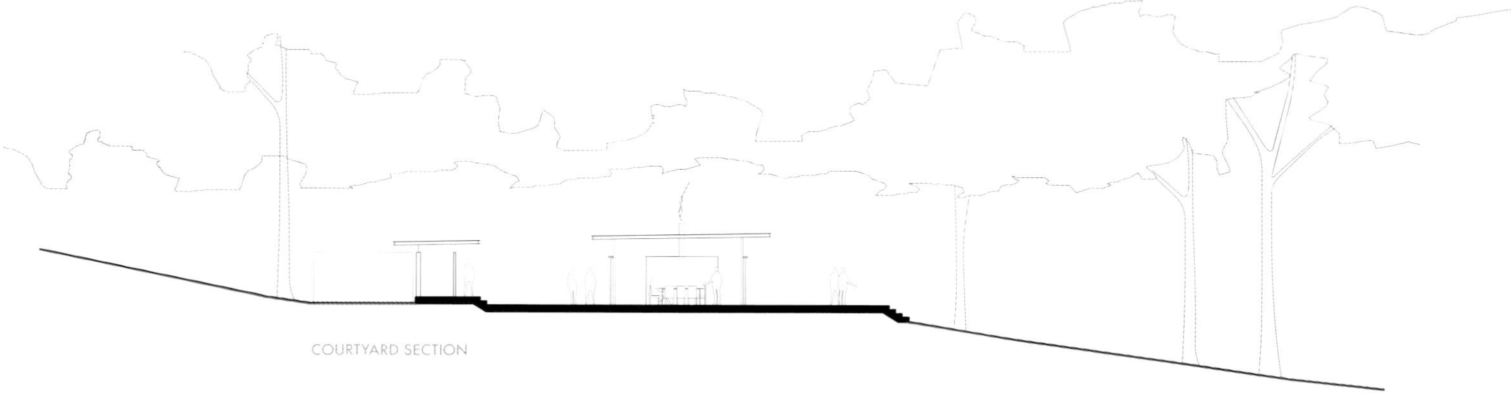

COURTYARD SECTION

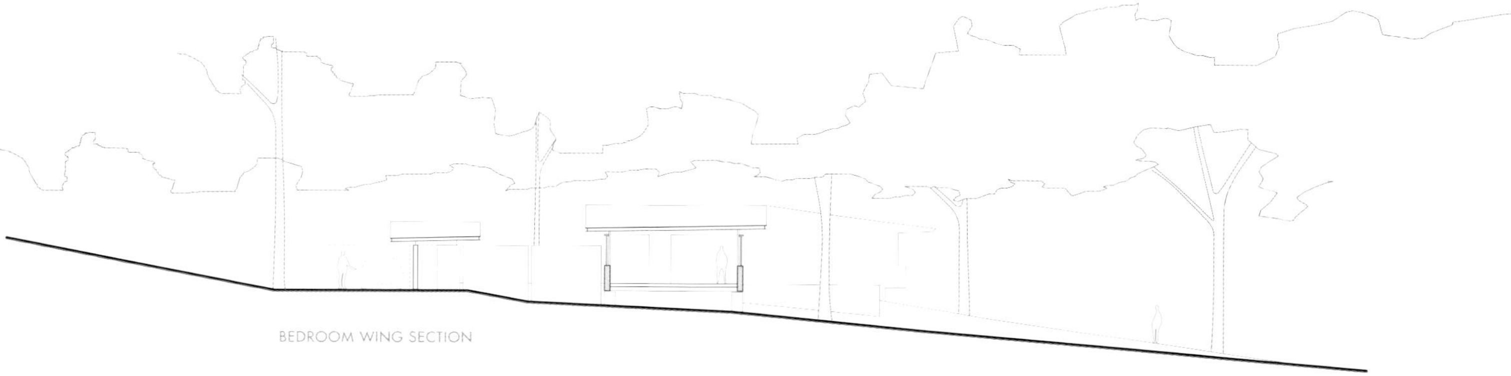

BEDROOM WING SECTION

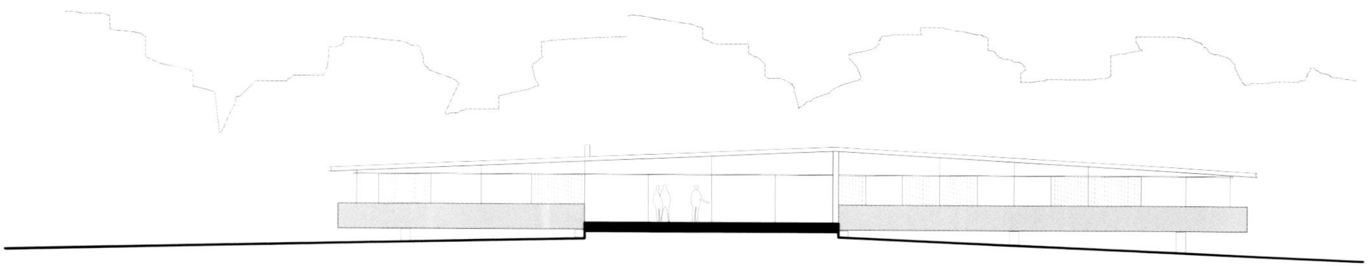

SOUTH ELEVATION

1 BEDROOM
2 CLOSET
3 BATH
4 LOUNGE
5 DINING
6 KITCHEN
7 STUDY
8 BATHROOM
9 RUMPUS ROOM
10 COURTYARD
11 STORAGE, MUDROOM, AND LAUNDRY
12 BATHROOM
13 POOL
14 CARPORT
15 TERRACE
16 DOUBLE-SIDED FIREPLACE

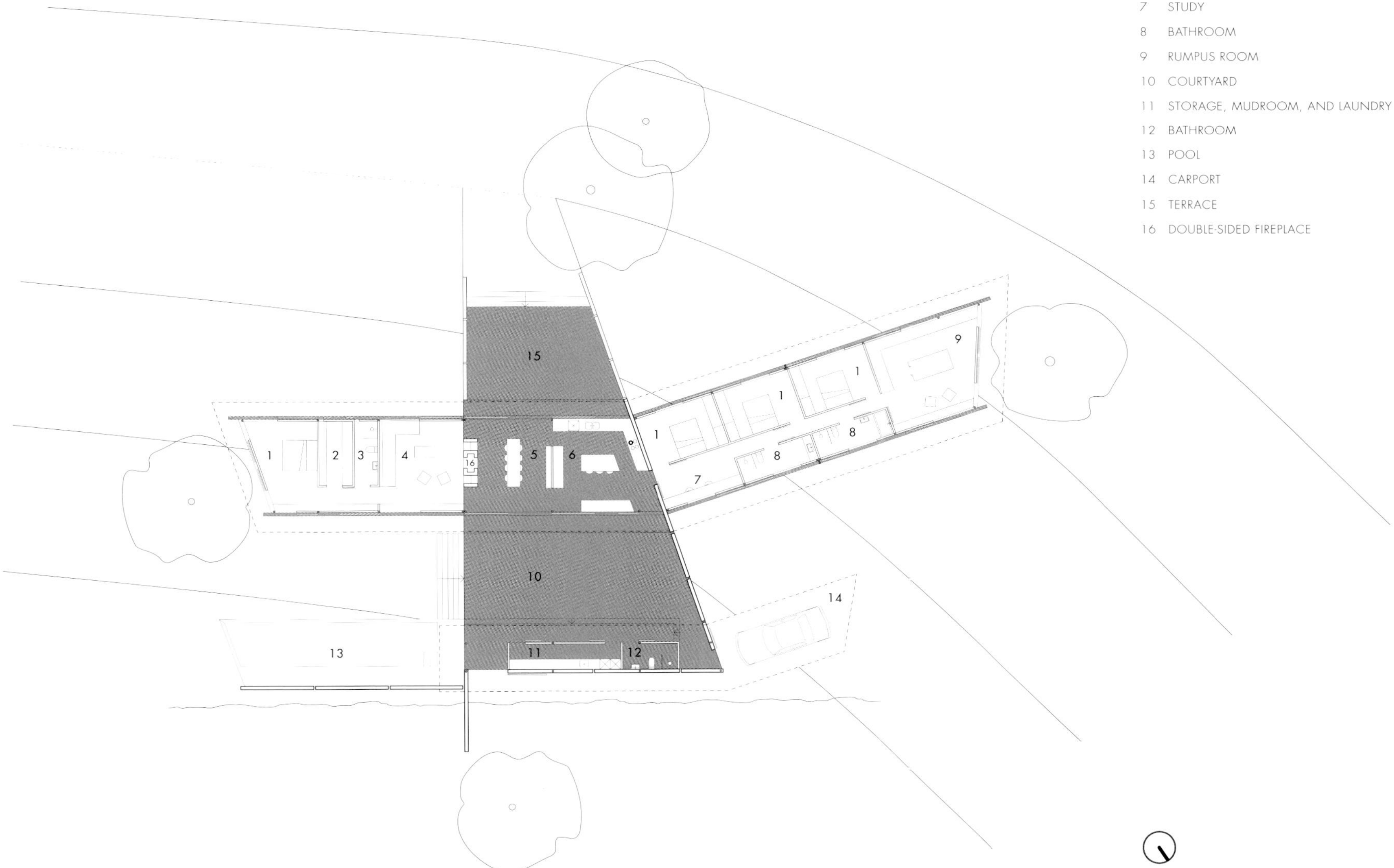

Bands of jarrah wood, the clerestory, and the flat roof draw a long horizontal line on the land. Only the center section rests on the ground, while the wings are on minimal pylons that can adjust to ground-surface shifts due to mining in the area.

SUNSET HOUSE

Inyadda Beach, New South Wales

Peter Stutchbury Architecture

6

In this small hamlet on the south edge of Australia, weather arrives in a tumultuous way, coming in from across the Pacific Ocean. So this wide-open building, on the spur of a windswept headland, had to be tough, especially on its east side facing the view. Designed as four porous pavilions under a single skylit roof, it intertwines with the landscape in a magical yet utilitarian way. The cambered roof changes bay by bay, and in the living area it becomes a pyramid folded down against the weather.

Under that sheltering roof, pebbled hallways connect the main living area to a bedroom, a storage room, and a service area along the south wall containing the trash bins, laundry, outdoor shower, and outdoor kitchen. In the walkout basement below, a private master bedroom and bath face the morning sun full-on through a canted glass wall. Here, with the dramatic drop-off to the sea, the house feels like a foothold in a rock, surrounded by big trees.

"The building comes off the top of the cliff as a series of two platforms," says architect Peter Stutchbury. "It comes off the top of the rock as masonry and turns into timber as it gets farther away from the rock base, not dissimilar to the way a tree is anchored to the top of a landform."

Designed as a single story when seen from the street, the camp-like concrete block, wood, and glass structure is open on the north side with gardens and courtyards, and shut down on the south, where bad weather comes from. Decks and walkways direct views to the sea. "The house is sited around a grove of casuarina trees that sing when the wind comes through, so as you enter the building, you go past a storeroom that can be converted into a bedroom with a sink and access to the bath," Stutchbury says. "Along the walkway, there is a view down the beach to the trees, and invariably, the northeast breeze is blowing; the music changes based on the velocity of the wind."

Sometimes used as an Airbnb, the house withstands hard use but is "nurturing in the way it accommodates the qualities of the site, and therefore the spiritual nature of the place," Stutchbury says. "It aims its primary living body to the sunrise but has a sunset room where you go for a quieter environment well out of the wind. It's almost like a segment of music that has all the variations in terms of instruments, intensity, pause, silence. All those qualities exist from west to east along the building. You choose your habitation depending on climate and weather. In summer they live in the courtyards; in winter they move to the northern edges of the building." During the frigid winters, the roofline allows the sun to come in from the north and heat the concrete slab, while providing shade in summer, when the sun is higher in the sky.

"The main word for our designs is connection, that a building is connecting the clients to place, to themselves, and to a world beyond the place," Stutchbury says. "We try to design buildings that lift people's spirits."

‹ "Houses in Aussie villages were single level to the street, which presented a beautiful streetscape," Stutchbury says. Sunset House was built with timber cut from a sustainable forest, recycled-wood doors and windows, and a composite zinc roof that resists salt. Beneath the gravel courtyard at the entry is a 30,000-liter (8,000-gallon) rainwater collection tank. The light-colored, rounded pebbles reflect light and are easy to walk on; concrete stepping stones are turned upside down to show the texture.

A cave and a camp: The building is broken into pavilions but covered with one roof so you can walk from place to place out of the weather. The south wall contains trash bins, an outdoor shower area, and an outdoor kitchen.

With a loft above the kitchen area and a Murphy bed in the storeroom, the two-bedroom house can sleep up to twelve people.

THE ENDLESS SUMMER

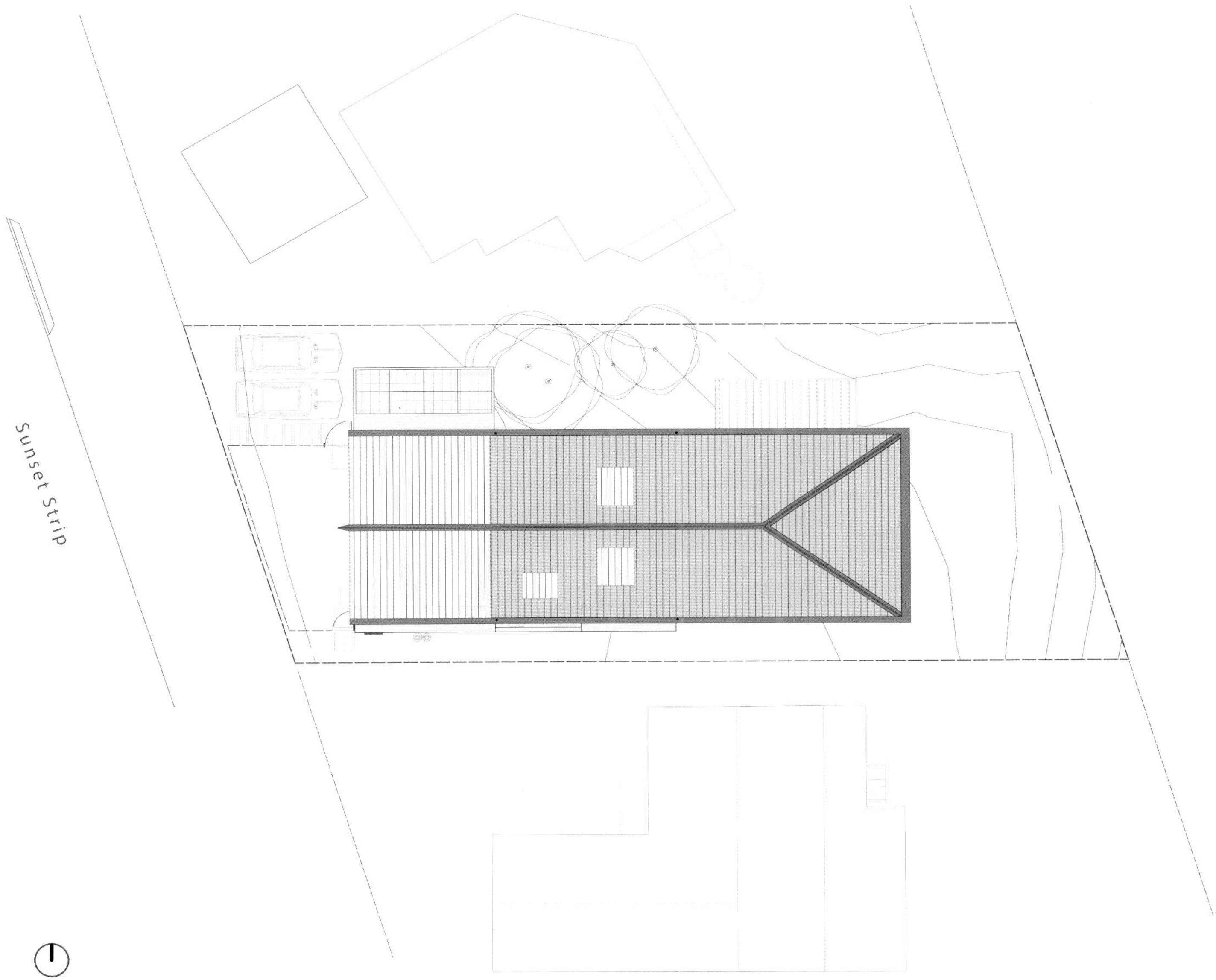
Sunset Strip

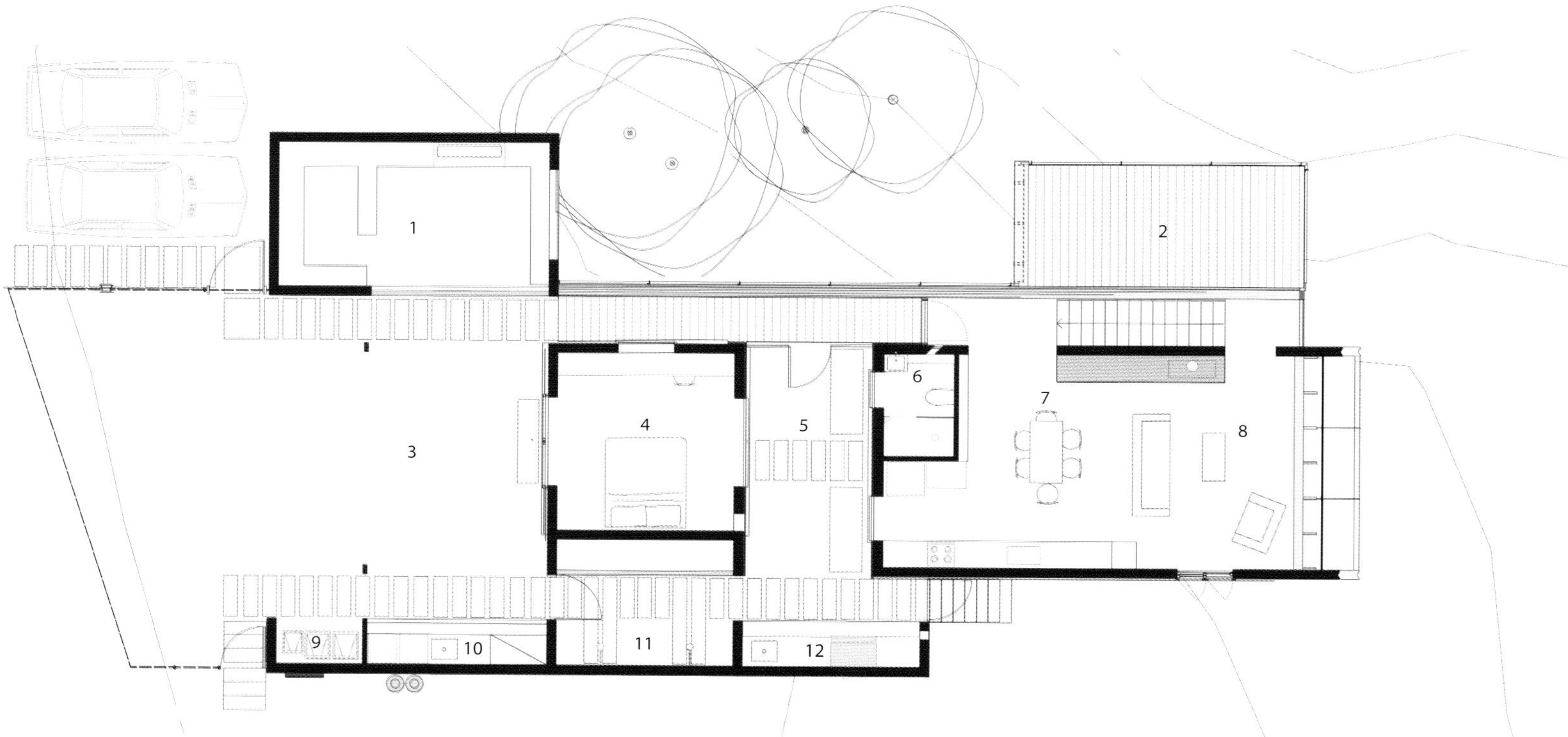

FIRST FLOOR PLAN

1 STORAGE
2 DECK
3 FRONT GARDEN
4 BEDROOM
5 COURTYARD
6 WASH
7 KITCHEN
8 LIVING
9 BINS
10 LAUNDRY
11 SHOWER
12 BBQ
13 WATER TANK
14 DRESSING ROOM

LOWER FLOOR PLAN

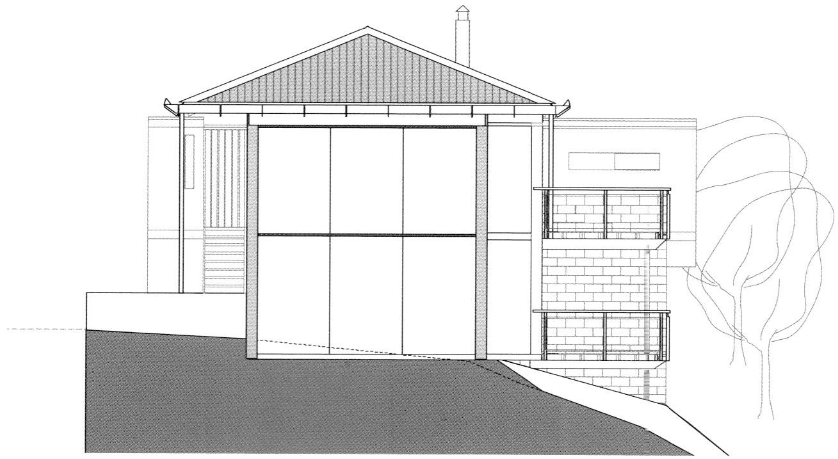

EAST ELEVATION

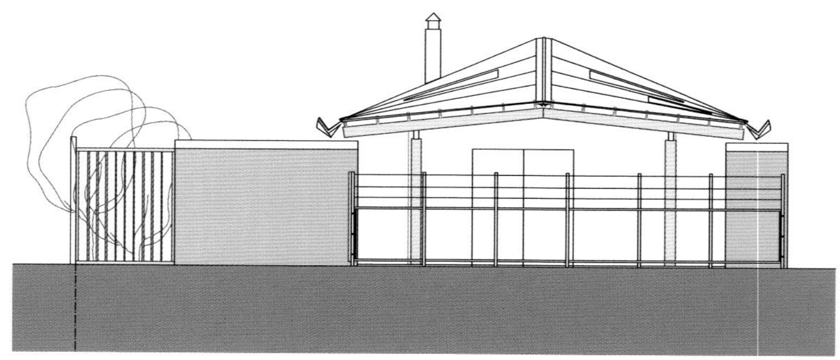

WEST ELEVATION

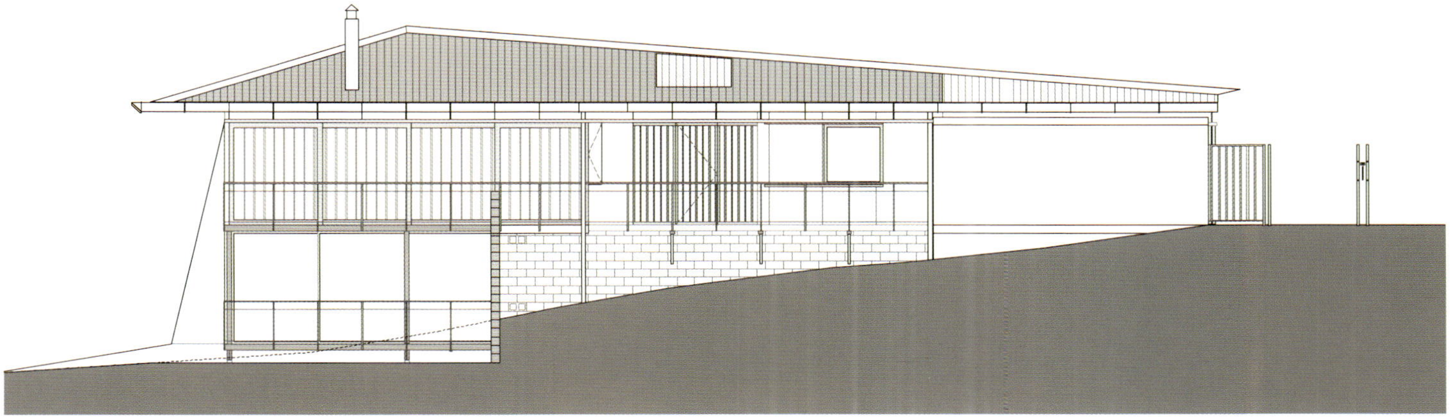

NORTH ELEVATION

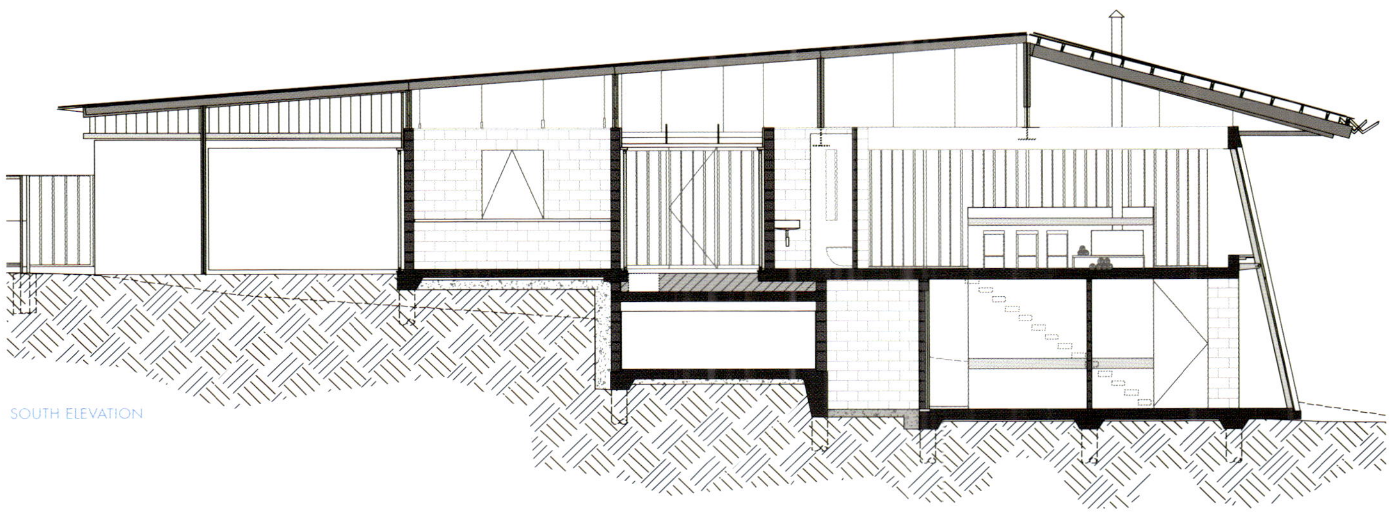

SOUTH ELEVATION

"The house is sited around a grove of casuarina trees that sing when the wind comes through. Along the walkway, there is a view down the beach to the trees, and invariably, the northeast breeze is blowing; the music changes based on the velocity of the wind."

NIKKI MALONEY HOUSE

Marrickville, New South Wales

7

Drew Heath Architects

Basic materials and quirky details went into remaking an old cottage in a middle-income neighborhood built between the 1900s and 1960s. Typically suburbs are on a grid, but a remnant road running through Marrickville resulted in this house's triangular lot that narrows in the back. "You find that a lot in Australia," says architect Drew Heath. "Presettlement tracks run into the overlaid grid and you get these leftover pieces that sometimes make for interesting sites."

Well known for his enthusiastically small, economical houses, Heath's design for this 1,345-square-foot house contains about 30 percent recycled materials, but it's not a patchwork. "I grew up working in timber and hardware stores, and to me, everything is a series of parts," says Heath, whose firm also builds the houses. "When I broke the house down I categorized it into basic parts, such as raw timber and bricks, that could be used for anything. But I set about designing the piece of architecture I had in mind regardless of the materials at hand."

The C-shaped footprint pays its respects to the street with a one-story front facade and gabled roof. But behind it, two double-level wings face off across a sunny rear courtyard that brings light into the middle of the structure. The deep incision in the footprint draws in cool, fresh air that gets pulled up the stairs to create a chimney effect. The garden insinuates itself into the upper level, too, where plants in boxes under the swooping roofs create privacy outside the two bedrooms and will eventually cascade over the walls. The courtyard incision borrows a view of two church spires on the east and west—one glimpsed from the kitchen through a circular cutout in the second-story roof.

The dialogue between inside and out, present and past, occurs on an unusually small level of detail, such as the light fittings with recycled bits and pieces. Even the cacti were bundled into pots and later replanted in the front yard. "We didn't have a lot of recycled materials because it was a very small cottage, so I tried to use them in places where they can be seen, touched, and talked about," Heath says. The front door is made out of the original flooring, and ironbark shingles from the underside of the roof reappear on a panel near the front door. Hardwood siding was repurposed as a front fence. "We left it raw, showing nail holes and patches where it had come off the timber frame," Heath says.

Even in the suburbs, this cozy, comfortable house harmonizes with the movement of sun, wind, air, and water. The stairs act as a thermal chimney, drawing cool air from across the courtyard pond and up through the house. Solar panels provide the house with electrical power and hot water, and rainwater is captured for use in toilets, laundry, and irrigation.

‹ Drew Heath used recycled materials in places where they could be seen, touched, and talked about. Louvered screens were made from old Baltic pine.

› Violet-colored hardwood siding from the original cottage was repurposed as a front fence and left raw, showing nail holes and patches where it came off the wood frame.

"Nothing has a finish; everything is raw so it's a natural building, and it's all open so you're breathing fresh air."

"There's a certain fitness that comes with a small budget and an economy that makes the design. You have to be clever to make good architecture on a small budget and site and with a small amount of materials."

› Circular roof cutouts bring light into the middle of the building.

› The double-faced interior-exterior brickwork, with an insulation gap in the middle, came from a local demolition project. "With the C-shaped plan, you understand you're within this solid recycled material," Heath says.

"The fact is that when you pay for sorting, stripping, and cleaning the materials, you spend a little more, but for me the value is in the story and texture, and the moral issue of not putting the building in the tip. It's easy for the owner, who had lived there for many years, to then bring a story to the building that she understands and can tell."

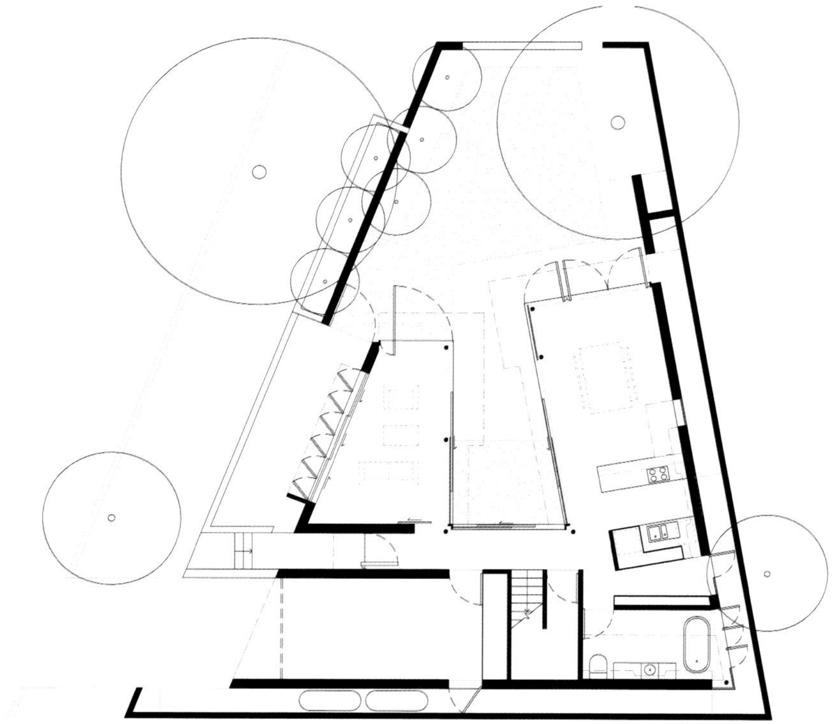

GROUND FLOOR PLAN

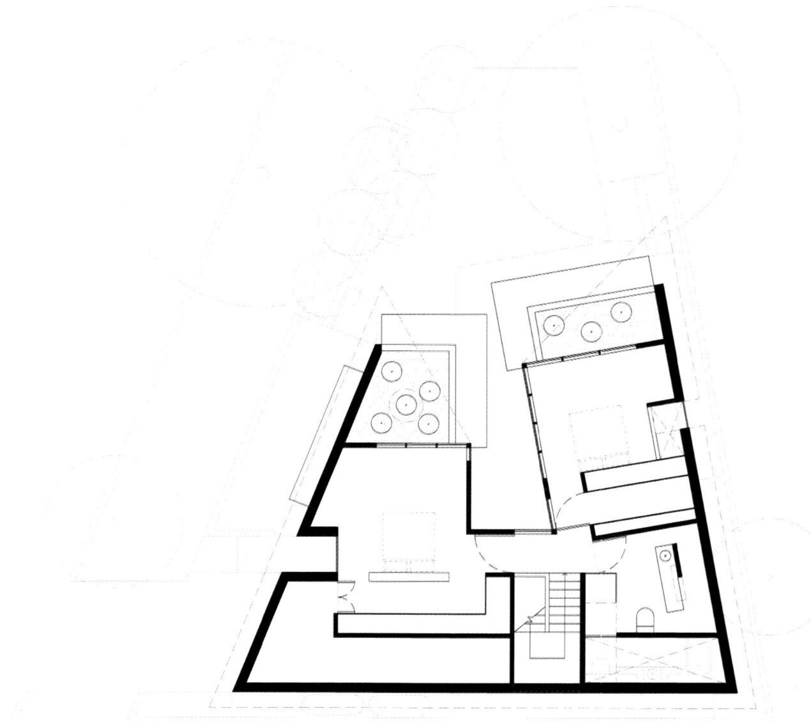

UPPER FLOOR PLAN

CHARLES HOUSE

Melbourne, Victoria

8

Austin Maynard Architects

In a neighborhood of McMansions and mock Georgian townhouses, this large, linear house is broken into separate parts to avoid dominating the street. Located on the southern edge of a long east–west lot, its horizontally aligned living spaces face the consistent northern sun and the garden, which rethinks the suburban backyard by running from the street to sports fields at the back of the site.

The owners wanted a house that would adapt to a growing family for the next twenty-five years and accommodate live-in grandparents in the near future. Practical, low maintenance, and light filled, it dematerializes the lines between inside and out.

Slate tile patterns—a nod to the Victorian, Federation, and Edwardian-period houses in the neighborhood—give each of the four volumes a distinct personality, while spotted gum timber cladding on the lower walls absorbs the impact of soccer balls and provides a gentler surface for people to brush up against. Occasionally the slate wraps into the void between two volumes. "Each of the patterns used on the various facades was recommended by the contractors from their years of experience," the architects note. "The beauty, skill, and detail usually lost to the sky up on the roof can be appreciated close-up."

The ground floor is flexible, with a music room that can become a granny flat with its own bath and wheelchair access to the garden. It connects to the main house across a glass-walled bridge that doubles as a study, and, outside, across a small pond. Three children's bedrooms and a play area for the two girls and a boy occupy most of the second floor, while the master suite's access over a bridge turns it into a private retreat space.

Sliding walls in the children's suite enable them to be as connected or as separated as they wish. Here, a section of perforated floor lets them spy on the stairwell, which occupies a slot between two volumes. The house is full of such magical secret openings and sleights of hand. "Wherever we could, we introduced a little patch or flap you can open and talk through or squeeze through," says principal Mark Austin. "On the stairwell, a hatch is hidden in the slate so you can call out to someone downstairs."

As playful as it is, the house works hard to be resource efficient. An underground cistern captures rainwater for irrigation, laundry, and toilets. Breezes across the two ponds cool the interiors through cross-ventilation, and the concrete slab floors are radiant heated. In addition to rooftop solar panels, the house is fitted with adjustable louvers to mitigate heat gain on the glass, and along the north side, yellow steel awnings are sized to stop the hot summer sun but allow the lower winter sun to penetrate the interior.

› Slate patterns lend distinct personalities to the four volumes of this house, designed for a family of five and grandparents who stay for long periods.

"We loved the lichen-covered slate roofs on many of the old Edwardian, Federation, and Victorian homes in the neighborhood and were keen to respond to and connect with this rich material history, without copying or creating a pastiche of the past."

‹ "Everywhere we could, we introduced a little patch or flap you can open or talk through—or squeeze through if you're small enough," says Mark Austin.

FIRST FLOOR PLAN

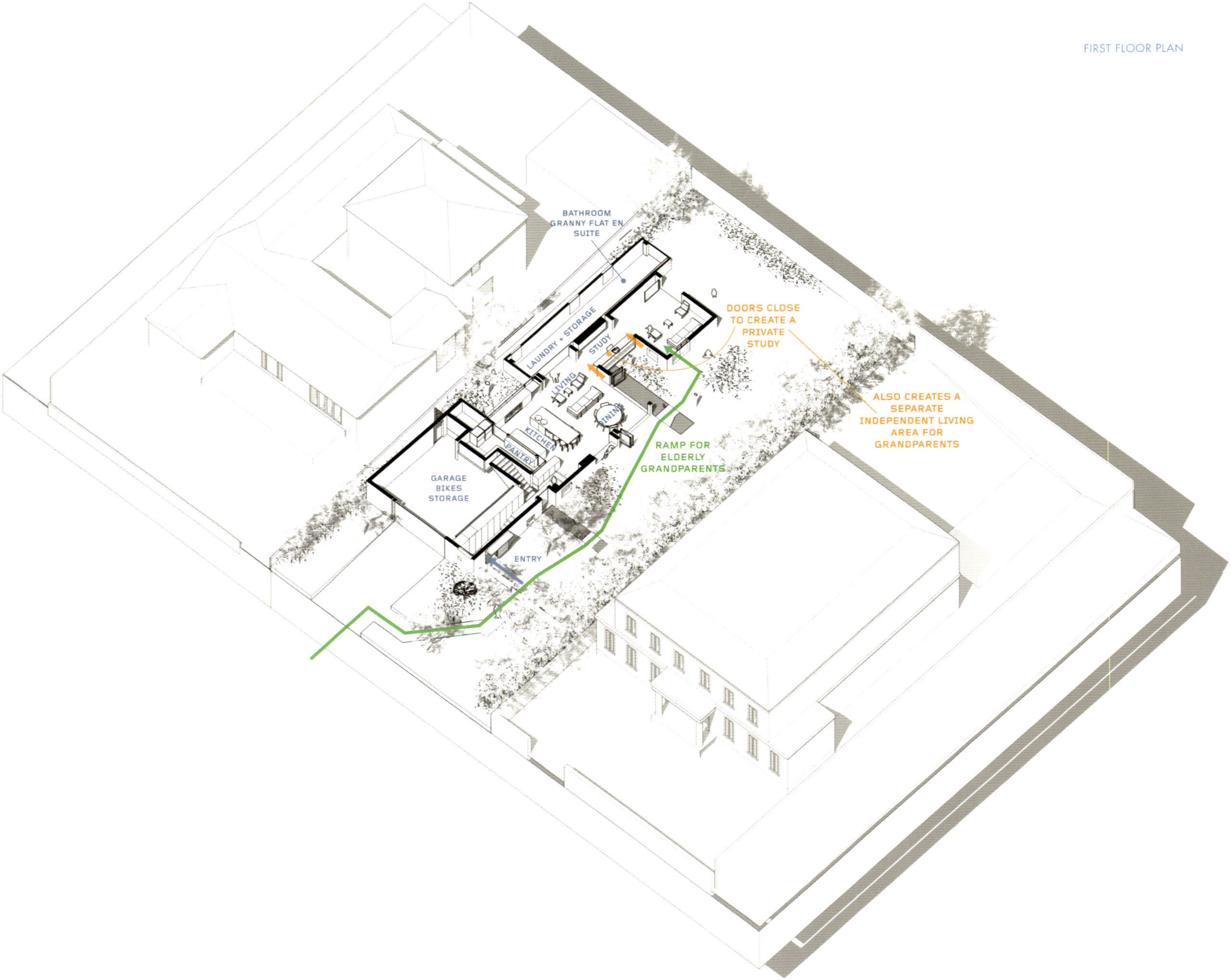

SECOND FLOOR PLAN

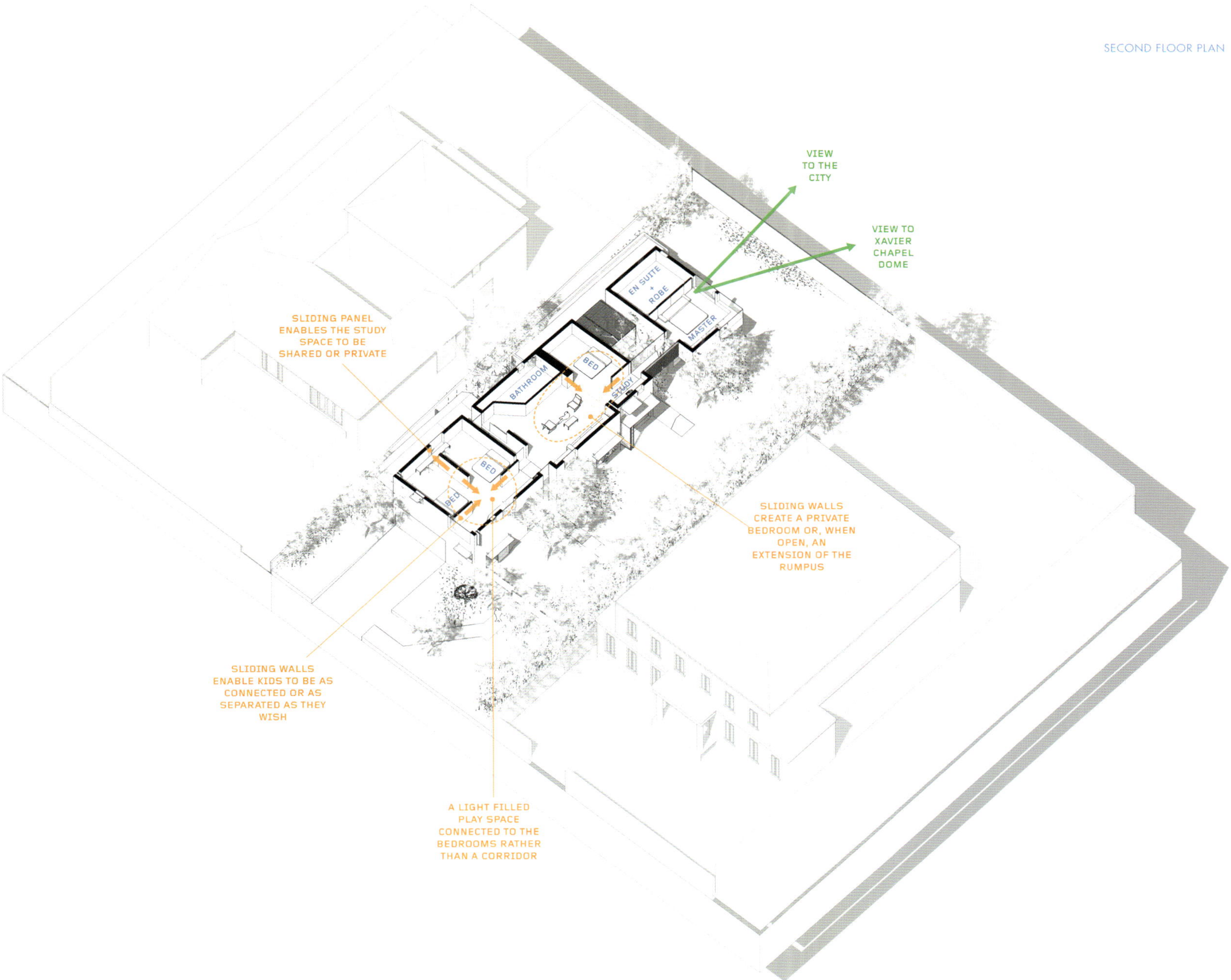

‹ Sliding panels open between the two girls' bedrooms.

‹ Yellow awnings face north to stop the hot summer sun but allow winter sun to warm the rooms.

15

COOGEE HOUSE II

South Coogee, New South Wales

9

Madeleine Blanchfield Architects

Often the most-alluring homes are the result of difficult conditions, whether they are economic or environmental. In this case it was the lot, which sloped steeply toward the back and was bookended by neighbors. "We knew it would have to step down the site and that we couldn't have a lot of side windows," says architect Madeleine Blanchard. "We came up with the idea of a central courtyard because the view of the ocean is at the back, and rooms could look through other rooms and get that view."

The long, axial, 300-square-meter (3,229-square-foot) plan responds directly to the climate and weather—and spectacularly to the light and view. Layers of open, glassy spaces step down with the land. At the heart of the house, the double-height courtyard separates the front section's guest room, laundry, and den from the dining/living/kitchen volume, which flows onto a rear terrace overlooking the pool. The north-facing courtyard, accessed through sliding doors on the dining room, hallway, and den, admits consistent sunlight, and adjacent rooms benefit indirectly through high windows. It is also a conduit for gentle cross-breezes from the northeast, while blocking the howling southeast wind. The house's upper level is set back from a green roof over the garage to preserve the street scale. Upstairs, laser-cut white fiber-cement folding screens filter out the hot direct sun and views into the bedrooms, emitting a soft glow at night.

Without a budget to execute materials to extreme precision, Blanchfield used rough-formed concrete and brick for the shell. The first floor's brick was layered unevenly to make it feel more textured, and painted white. Chunky timber-framed windows harmonize with the house's natural stone base, a material that was common on neighborhood bungalows in the 1930s and 1940s. "The owners are stone importers, so we had access to amazing stone that would have been out of budget," Blanchfield says. Custom-made terrazzo for the floors and marble for the kitchen and baths were shipped as enormous slabs from the owner's company in Italy.

With its balance between privacy and transparency, light and shadow, and natural ventilation and protection from the elements, the house becomes a living, breathing part of family life.

The main level steps down with the natural terrain while the ceiling height remains the same, opening the house to ocean views at the back. Indoor-outdoor rooms provide cross-viewing and cross-ventilation, allowing the family to experience the landscape from inside the house. The building responds to the climate with high windows, wind-protected courtyards, and sunscreens.

Terrazzo flooring holds the heat in winter; breezes whip through in summer, controlled by sliding doors.

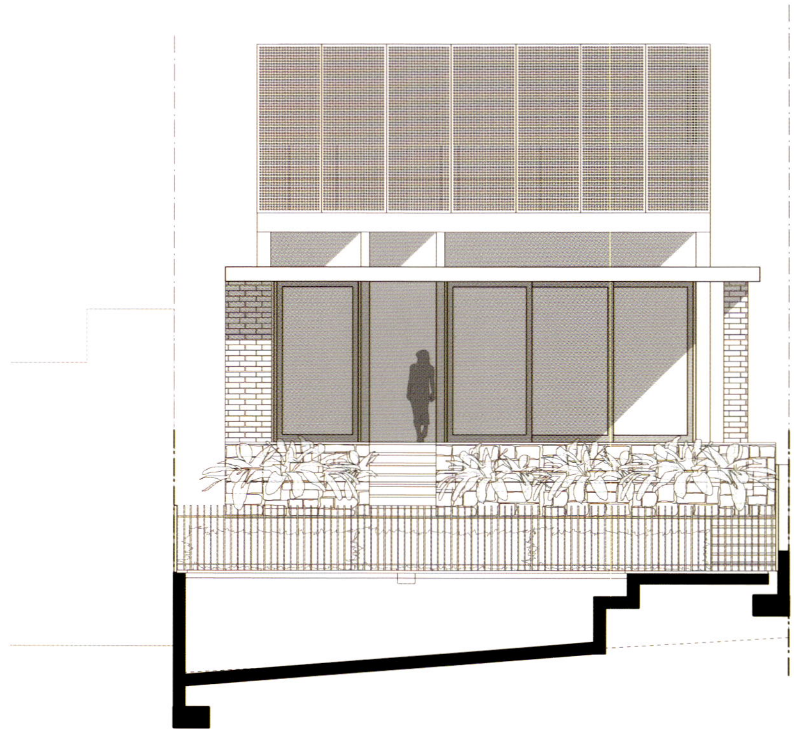

ELEVATIONS

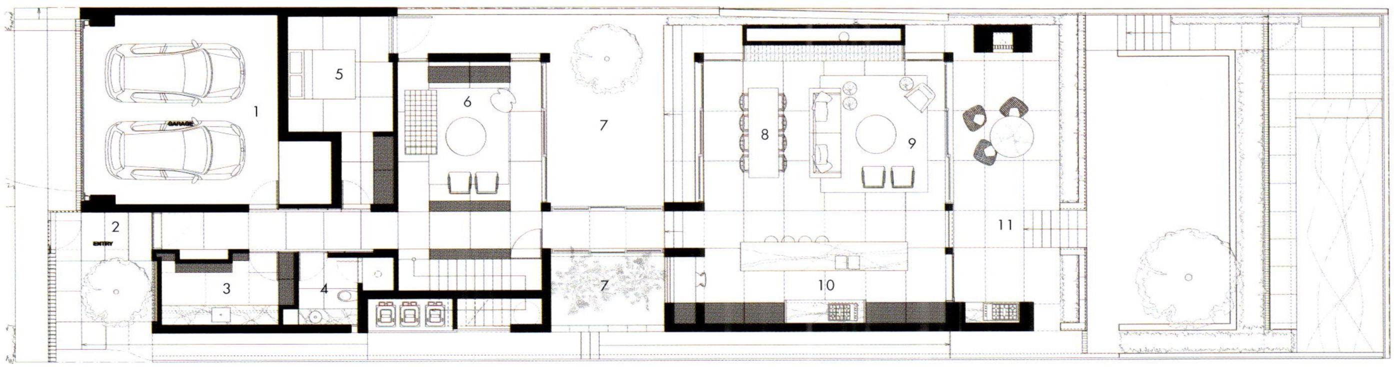

FIRST FLOOR PLAN

1 GARAGE
2 ENTRY
3 LAUNDRY
4 BATH
5 GUEST ROOM
6 RUMPUS
7 COURTYARD
8 DINING
9 LIVING
10 KITCHEN
11 TERRACE

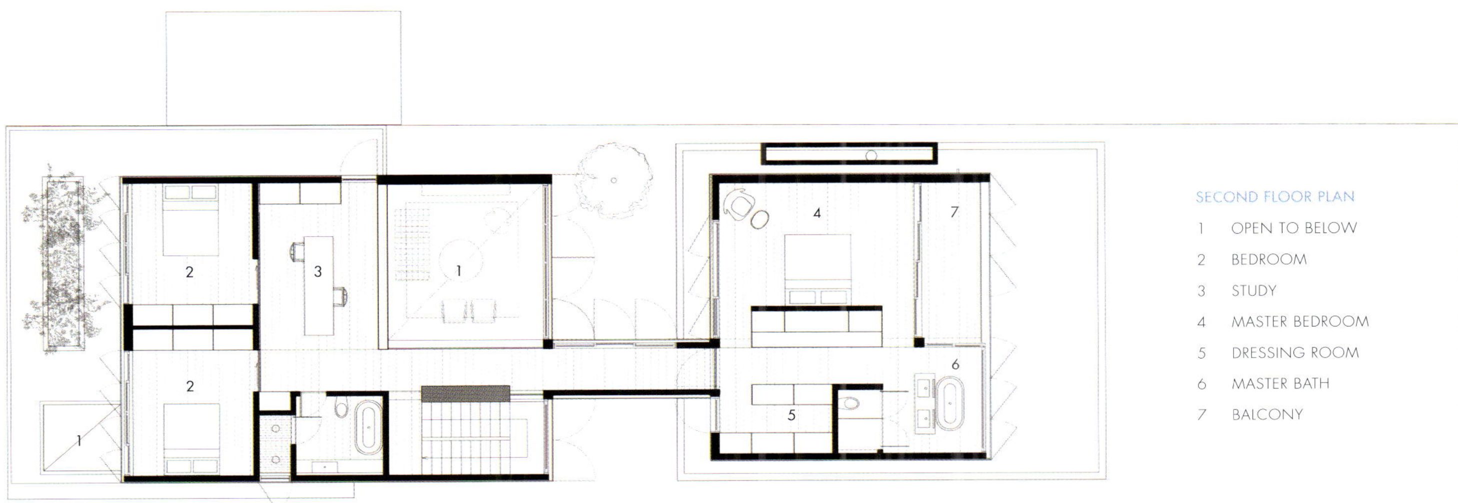

SECOND FLOOR PLAN

1 OPEN TO BELOW
2 BEDROOM
3 STUDY
4 MASTER BEDROOM
5 DRESSING ROOM
6 MASTER BATH
7 BALCONY

 Coogee House II, Madeleine Blanchfield Architects

› The first level's white brick was roughly layered to give it a textured effect that complements the stonework.

MOONLIGHT CABIN

Shipwreck Coast, Victoria

10

Jackson Clements Burrows Architects

Water, light, and landscape work in harmony in this cabin, near the Twelve Apostles on Victoria's west coast. It was designed for a man who used to camp near this tourist destination and wanted a place where he and his two children could sit and observe the wild, atmospheric landscape, which includes bits of remnant rainforest. The site is exposed to harsh winds; hence the outer layer of perforated shutters, which can be adjusted in response to different weather conditions.

Spotted gum timbers were used as a rain screen over a waterproof skin. They act like a breathable "Gore-Tex jacket" to protect the interior from the elements, while integral shutters can close down the cabin when the wind s blowing from the south or when the owner isn't there. "You can always see through them," says architect Tim Jackson, "and flywire on the inside stops insects and embers, in the event of a fire, from coming through."

Measuring only 60 square meters (645 square feet), the interior "is a bit like the husk of a seed pod," says Jackson. Victorian ash timber walls coated with lime lend a refined feel that contrasts with the rough outer shell. The various spaces float free of the wall—a clever circulation alternative to a space-hogging corridor. A built-in couch area is set up around the "campfire"—a hanging hearth. Behind it is a breakfast bar, and on the other side of the wall are a pair of bunk beds, a double bed, and a bathroom. At the other end of the cabin to the north, a galley kitchen opens to an indoor-outdoor veranda, "like the fly of a tent," where shutters can be opened or closed.

The cabin was designed as a glorified camping spot where the owner could sit and observe the wild, atmospheric landscape with his two children. Bath, bedrooms, living room, and kitchen line up to form the core, with circulation space around them.

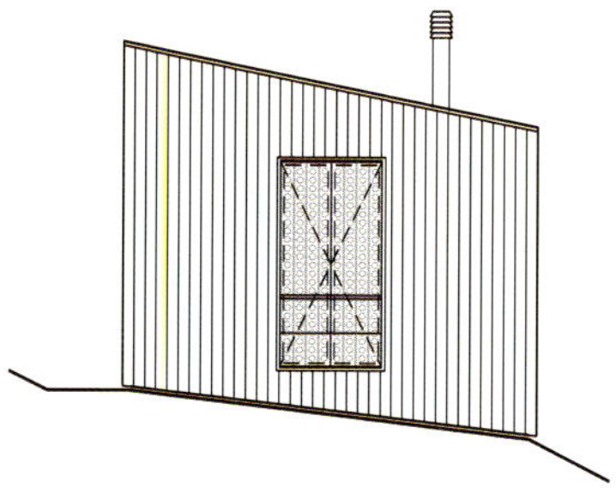

SOUTH ELEVATION

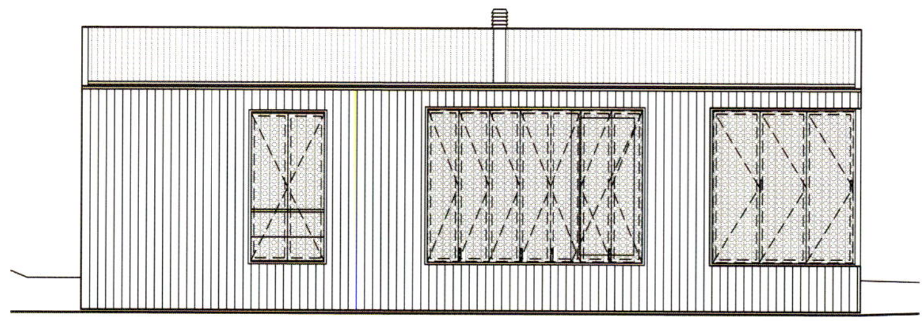

EAST ELEVATION

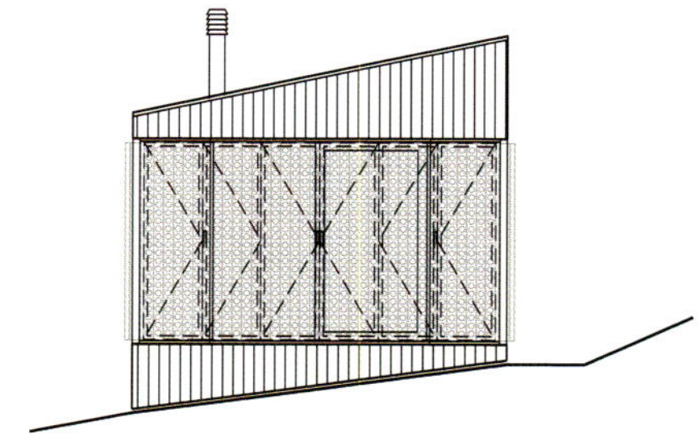

NORTH ELEVATION

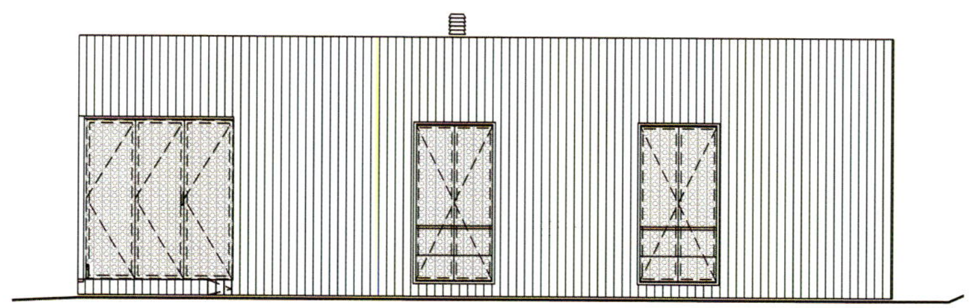

WEST ELEVATION

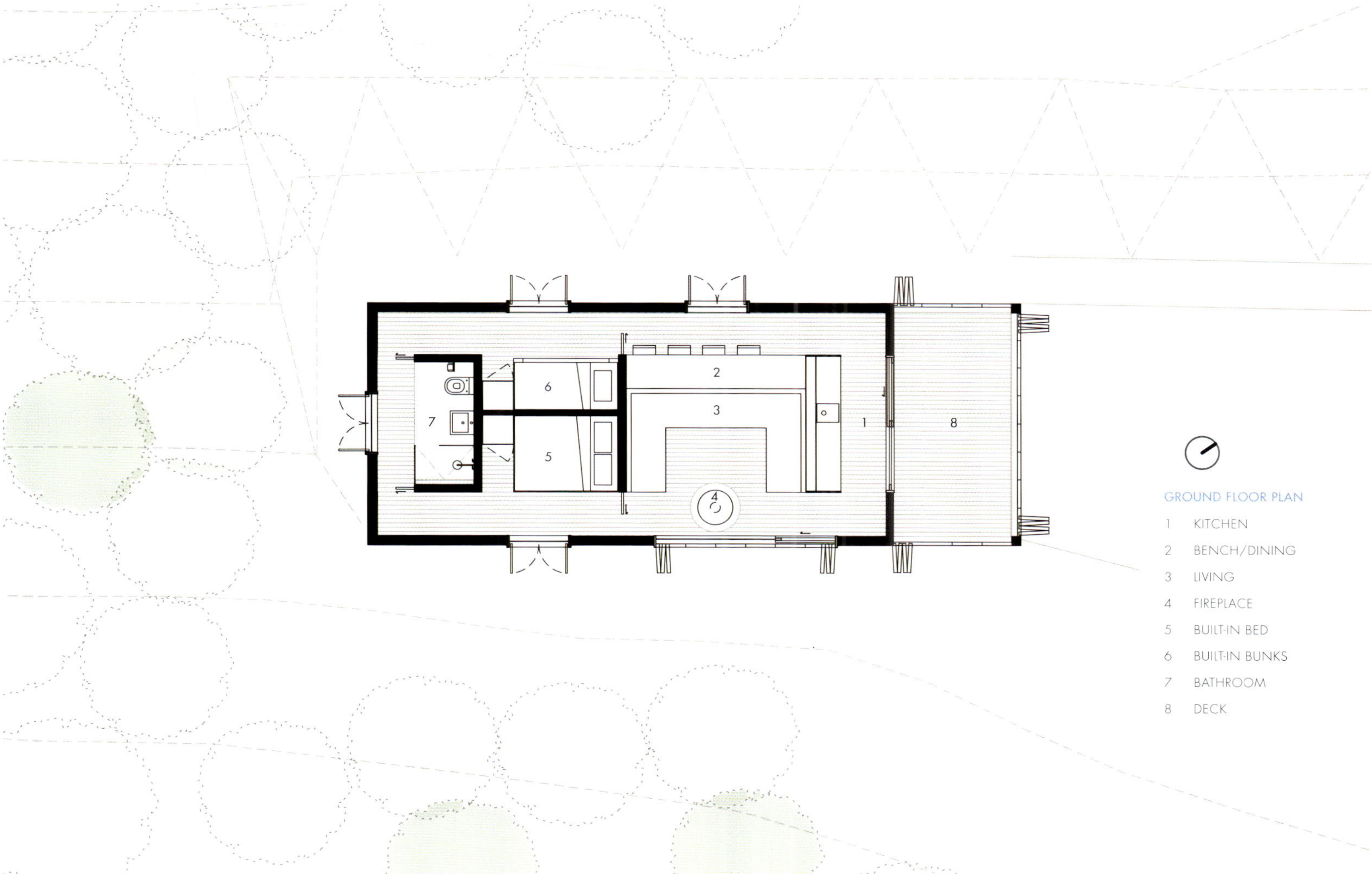

GROUND FLOOR PLAN

1 KITCHEN
2 BENCH/DINING
3 LIVING
4 FIREPLACE
5 BUILT-IN BED
6 BUILT-IN BUNKS
7 BATHROOM
8 DECK

SECOND VALLEY HOUSE

Second Valley, South Australia

11

Max Pritchard Architect

Shelter and exposure find poetic expression in this house in a valley, where hills rise up steeply on the east and west. The sweep of the roofline reflects this landform when seen from a distance. Summers in this coastal location, about 46 miles south of Adelaide, can be as hot as 100 degrees Fahrenheit, and wintertime temperatures can go down to 0, says architect Max Pritchard. With that in mind, he drew a long, thin plan and oriented it along an east–west axis to maximize winter sun and summer breezes—the house's main source of cooling. Its five bedrooms, family room, and large blackbutt deck are arrayed along the north side so that they bask in the sun all day, while the garage, utility rooms, courtyard entrance, and kitchen/dining/lounge area unspool along the south facade.

Visitors enter through a walled courtyard on the south, which shelters the house from strong winds. "It becomes an outdoor living area with a barbecue and is cool during the day in summer," Pritchard says. Inside, the material palette is plain and undetailed to defer to the views up the hills and to the sea. An old ruin on the property supplied some of the stone for the exterior, and more was sourced from other abandoned buildings nearby. Plywood panels at the garage and entrance add richness, while battens hide the joints and give the house a slightly Japanese look.

If the house has a grand quality owing to its dramatic roofline, the swoop also serves a utilitarian purpose by funneling rainwater into an 80,000-liter (21,134-gallon) aboveground tank, which supplies the household's water. Sensitively integrated with the prevailing weather and verdant topography, this house radically enhances the occupants' appreciation for the natural world—something every dwelling should do.

> The front door opens to a courtyard that shelters the house from winter winds and provides a cool place to relax outdoors in summer.

‹ Interior materials are modest and minimally detailed to let the view take center stage.

^ Timeless, hundred-year-old stonework came from a ruin on the site and nearby abandoned buildings.

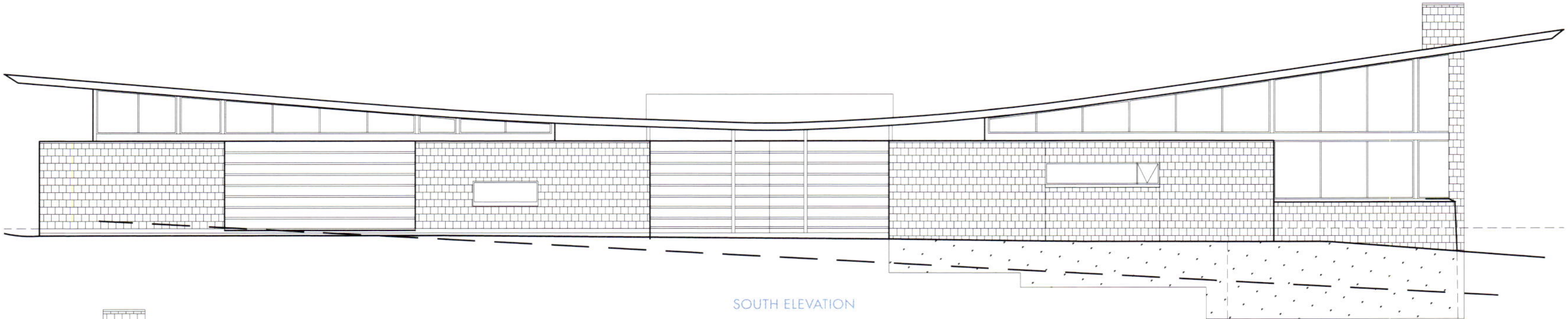

SOUTH ELEVATION

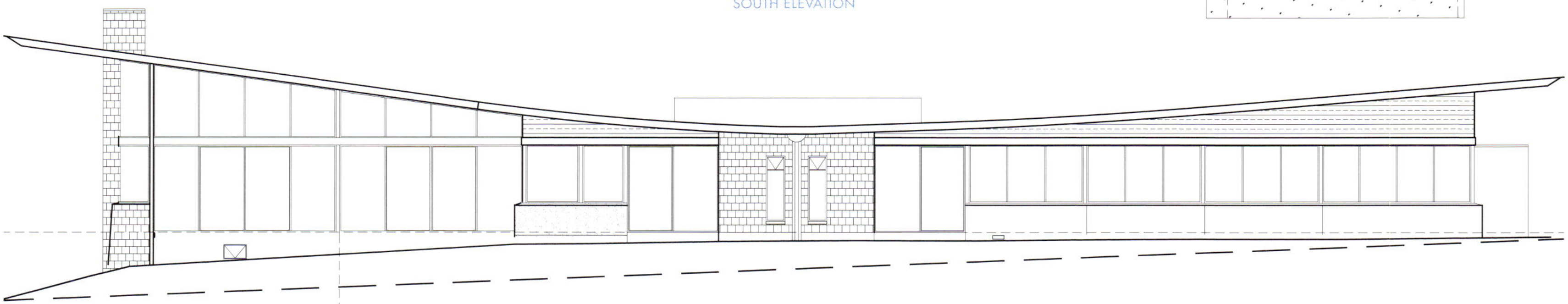

NORTH ELEVATION

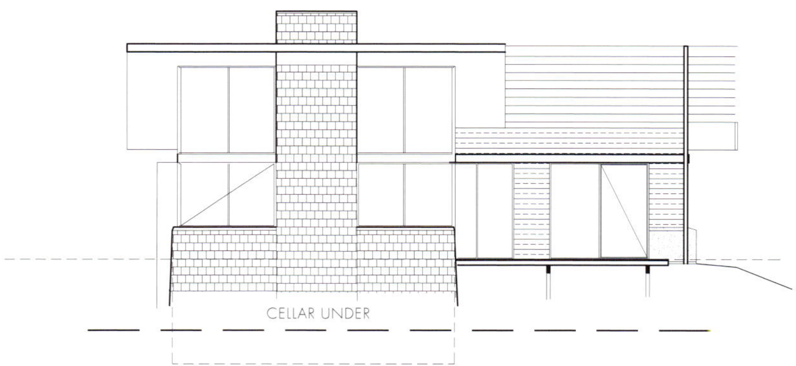

EAST ELEVATION

WEST ELEVATION

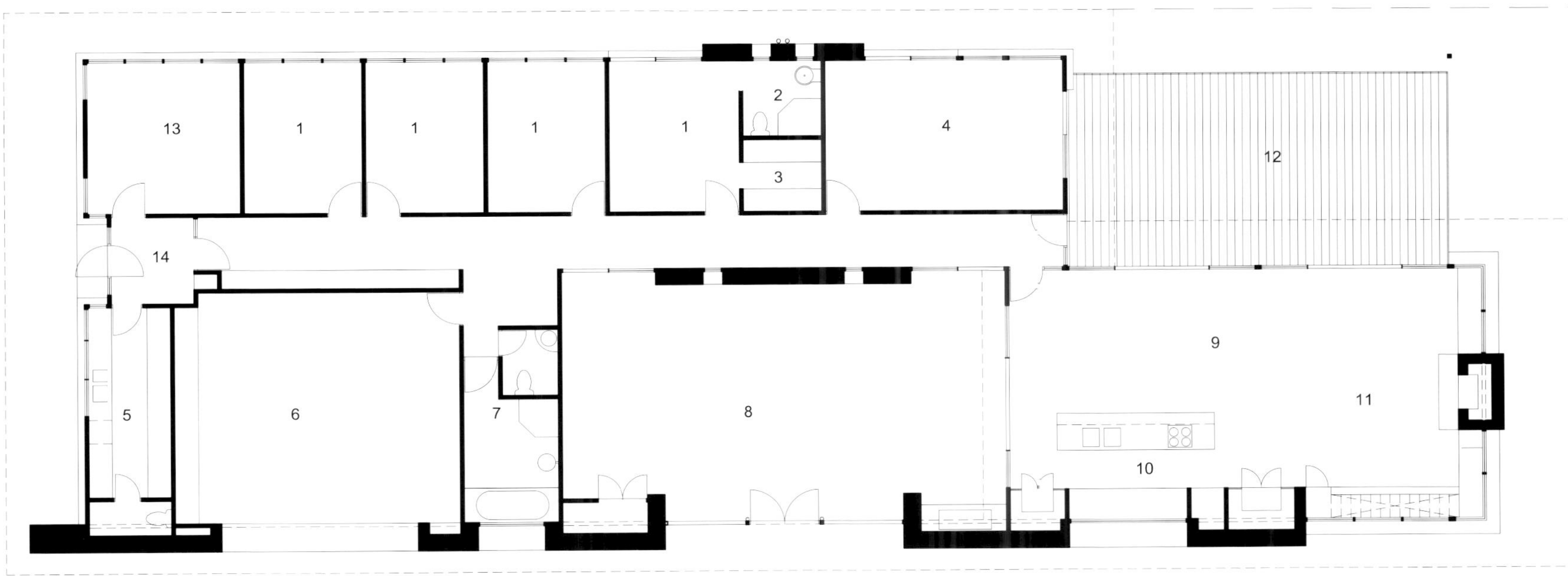

1 BED
2 BATH
3 DRESSING ROOM
4 FAMILY ROOM
5 LAUNDRY
6 GARAGE
7 BATH
8 COURTYARD
9 DINING
10 KITCHEN
11 LIVING
12 TERRACE
13 OFFICE
14 SIDE ENTRY

‹ The pergola was designed for deciduous vines to provide shade in summer, but the owners preferred its unadorned drama. The decking is blackbutt, a hardwood that resists fire.

HOUSE MAHER

Sydney, New South Wales

12

Tribe Studio Architects

Limned in light, this house in a leafy suburb connects to the outdoors in a lyrical way, despite its classic lines. As simple as a child's drawing, it responds to the neighborhood of primarily Federation and 1920s dwellings. Tribe Studio based its pitched-roof outline on the lot's existing bungalow, which was torn down to create a house that would allow the wife, who uses a wheelchair, to be as independent as possible.

The front and rear facades are clad in recycled bricks salvaged from the original house for their thermal qualities and reference to the surrounding homes. But if the outside reads as a simple, peaked volume, the interior is full of light, air, and unexpected views. The entry hall, flanked by the master suite and a second bedroom, opens into a cathedralized dining and living room, where a large window high on the gable end brings light deep into the plan.

Upstairs (wheelchair accessible by elevator), a series of pitched interior planes define the TV room, study, and bedrooms three and four—houses within a house. Roof skylights and cutaways in the plasterboard walls open sight lines to the sky, garden, and first floor.

The interior's calm, relaxed demeanor is supported by cross-ventilation and operable skylights at the highest point in the two-story spaces, which create a chimney effect to draw out hot air. Nor'easterlies blow over the pool and into the house, further cooling it in summer. Rainwater is harvested and recycled to the toilets, laundry, and garden.

This project is an example of how suburban conventions can be updated and adapted to serve specific needs, and how a house can imaginatively fuse old and new. "We believe individual houses have a responsibility to enhance the wider context," says firm principal Hannah Tribe. "Every house we design, large or small, is a picture of the client we work with. In reflecting their personalities, values, and interests, it is a form of portraiture."

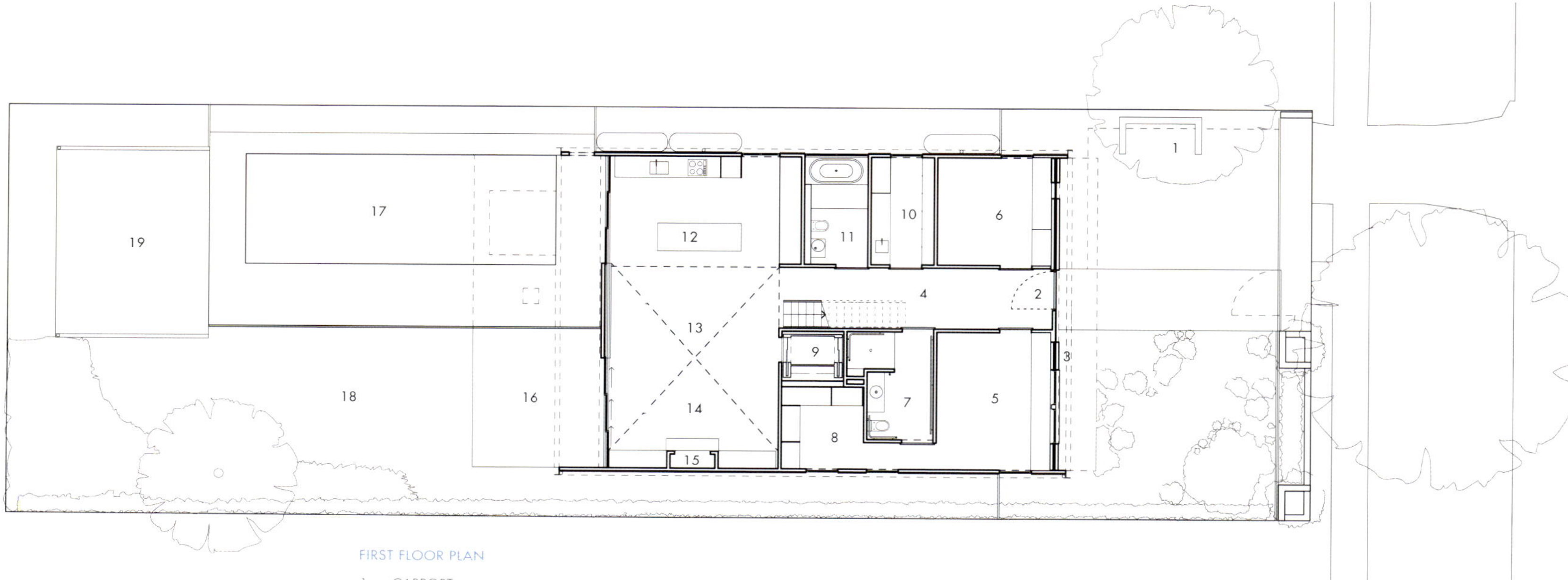

FIRST FLOOR PLAN

1 CARPORT
2 ENTRY
3 TRASH BINS
4 HALLWAY
5 MASTER BEDROOM
6 BEDROOM
7 MASTER BATHROOM
8 DRESSING ROOM
9 LIFT
10 LAUNDRY
11 BATHROOM
12 KITCHEN
13 DINING
14 LIVING
15 FIREPLACE
16 DECK
17 POOL
18 GARDEN
19 GRANNY FLAT

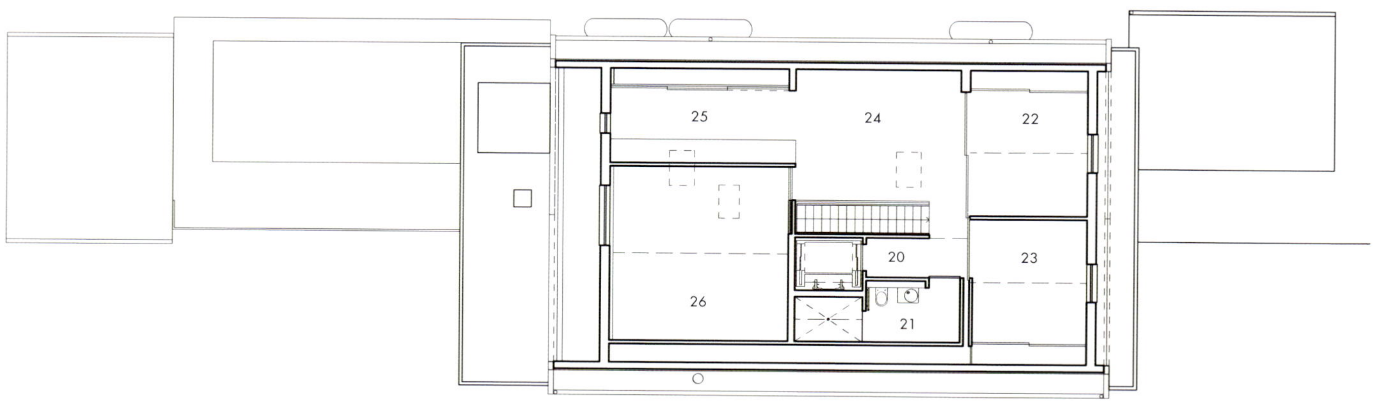

SECOND FLOOR PLAN

20 HALLWAY
21 BATH
22 BEDROOM
23 BEDROOM
24 TV ROOM
25 STUDY
26 VOID

CROSS SECTION 1

4 HALLWAY
5 MASTER SUITE
6 BEDROOM 2
22 BEDROOM 3
23 BEDROOM 4

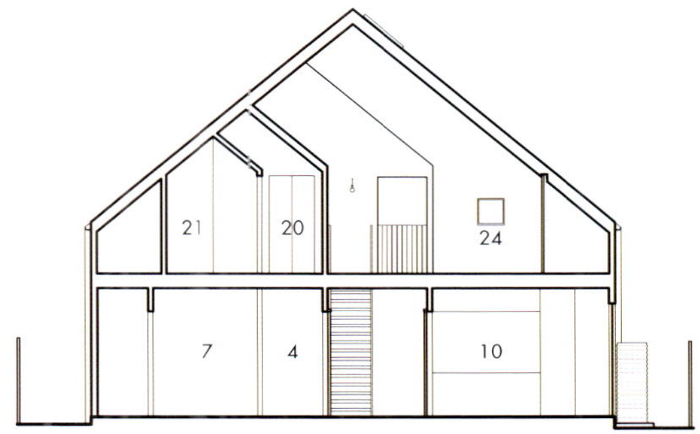

CROSS SECTION 2

4 HALLWAY
7 MASTER BEDROOM
10 LAUNDRY
20 HALLWAY
21 BATHROOM
24 TV ROOM

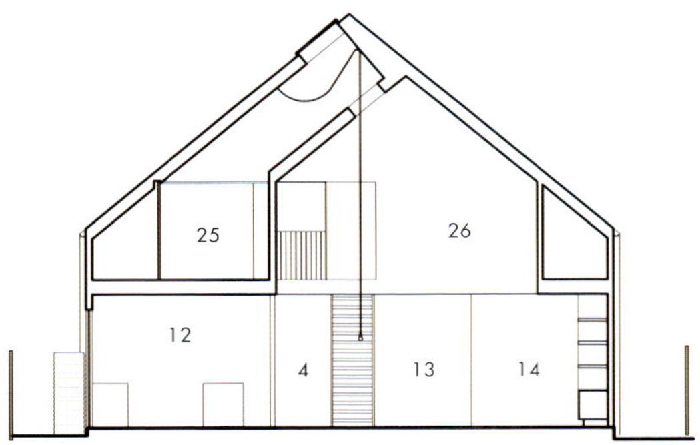

CROSS SECTION 3

4 HALLWAY
12 KITCHEN
13 DINING
14 LIVING
25 STUDY
26 VOID

REAR ELEVATION

57

FRIEDRICHSTRASSE HOUSE

Maylands, South Australia

13

Troppo Architects

^ The house was built virtually on the lot line to carve out space for private interior courtyards.

This house sits in a conservation zone where any new construction must respect the character of the neighborhood's older bungalows. Architect Phil Harris's design blends in, "but you just know something else is going on," he says.

That "something else" is the result of using the entire lot (after a lengthy approvals process) to create light-filled interior and exterior living spaces—"the site becomes the house," Harris says. No space is wasted on this long, narrow plot. Its three pavilions—office/entry/garage, kitchen/dining/lounge, and master suite—are separated by two courtyards carved out on the north side, facing the sun. A continuous south wall made of rammed earth provides thermal mass on the "weather" side of the house while containing the service functions—laundry, bath, and air-conditioning unit, which is needed only in extreme heat thanks to good cross-ventilation.

Passive cooling comes from clerestory windows that draw out hot air, and aluminum louvers—external Venetian blinds—that can be pulled up and down. "With climate change, we find the weather is so much wilder," Harris says. "With incredibly hot summer days, fixed sun shading doesn't work as well as having a dynamic method. This is an old tradition, which we still use."

To reduce maintenance time and costs, Harris chose materials that age gracefully and require no further finish. In addition to rammed earth, galvanized steel was used for the roof and some of the wall cladding, along with raw cement sheets. The porch roof is made of translucent polycarbonate, perforated to bounce just the right amount of light into the office from the front yard. With its variety of intertwined indoor-outdoor spaces, Harris calls the home "a rambling nest" with "distant places to drift off to"—a "palace on a postage stamp."

RALEIGH

A high window looks above the neighbors toward the hills, and the roof is inclined at the perfect angle for solar panels.

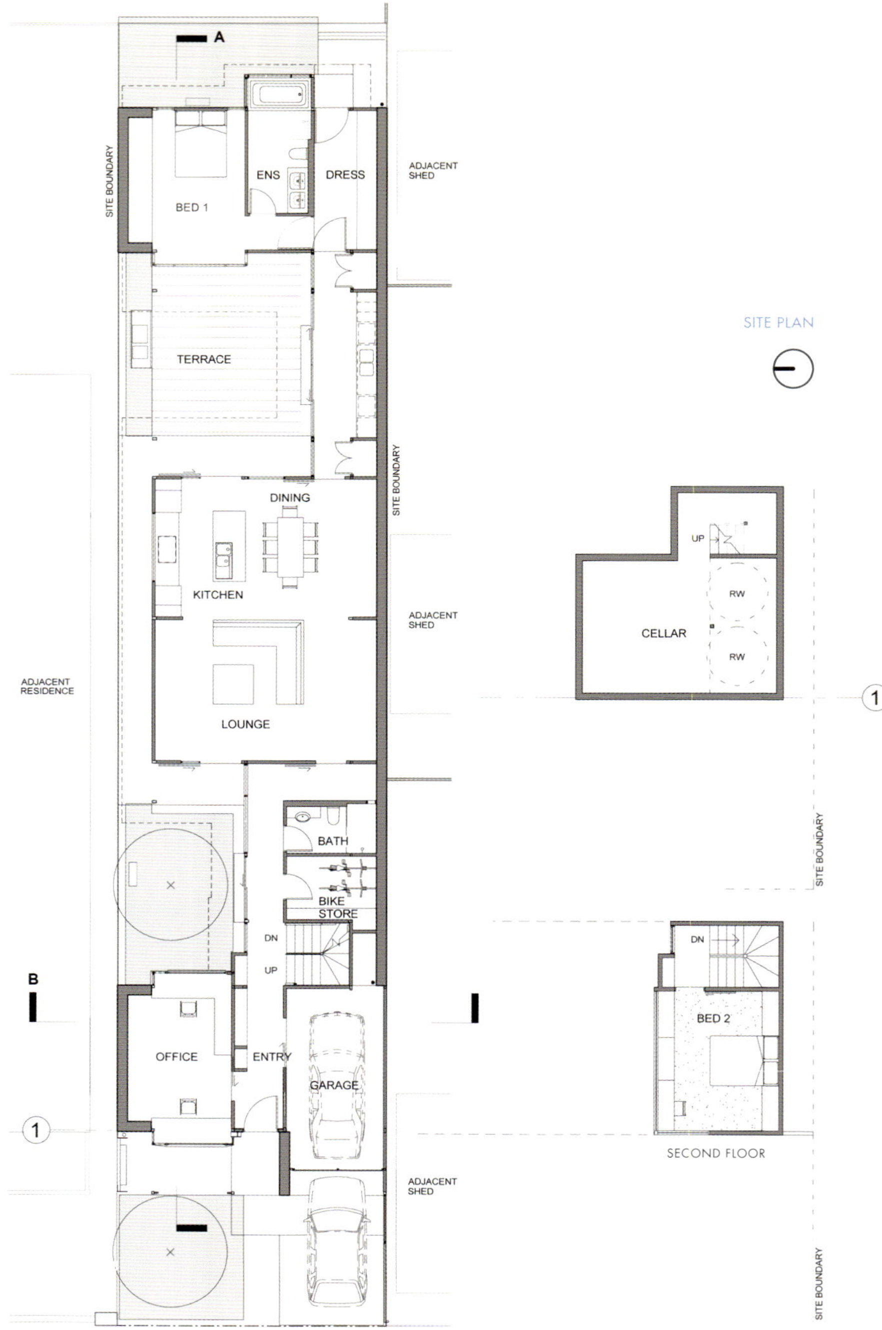
A
ENS
DRESS
BED 1
SITE BOUNDARY
ADJACENT SHED
TERRACE
SITE PLAN
DINING
KITCHEN
LOUNGE
ADJACENT SHED
ADJACENT RESIDENCE
SITE BOUNDARY
UP
RW
CELLAR
RW
1
BATH
BIKE STORE
DN
UP
B
OFFICE
ENTRY
GARAGE
1
DN
BED 2
SECOND FLOOR
ADJACENT SHED
SITE BOUNDARY
SITE BOUNDARY

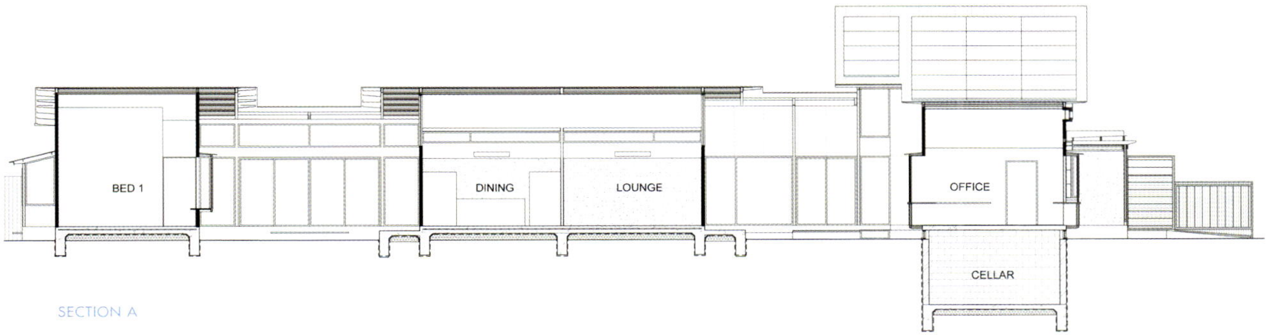

SECTION A

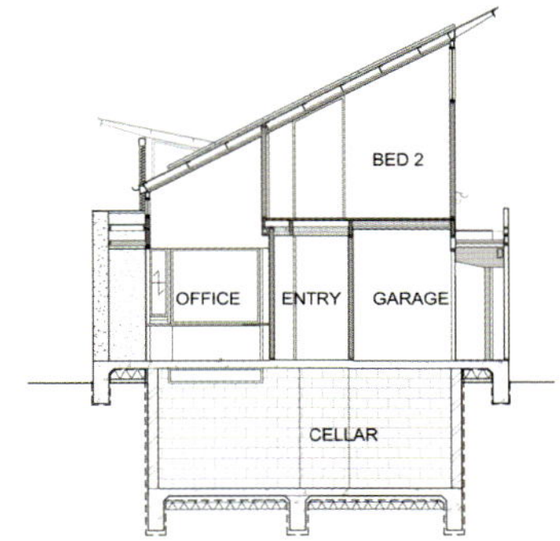

SECTION B

WEST ELEVATION

Vittoria
Coffee

INFILL
THE SOLAR HOUSE
scandimodern
NARROW HOUSES
Oxford CONCISE AUSTRALIAN DICTIONARY
PHILOSOPHY
Stephanie Alexander

CYCLES METEORE

WOLF HOUSE

Melbourne, Victoria

14

Wolf Architects

The Wolf House is above all a family house. With its ten subtle level changes, built-in collections of art and objects, and central ceremonial dining area, it is meant to be a "memory box" and a place for discovery, says architect Taras Wolf, who designed it for his young family of five. What's more, it can comfortably house them for twenty to thirty years if necessary. "Flexibility was extremely important; we find that a lot of young houses, fifteen years old, are being renovated, and it's a lot of waste," Wolf says.

The couple grew up in Southeast Asia, so the house has some East-meets-West sensibilities, including the playful Chinese garden that welcomes visitors at the front door. A bridge over a dry riverbed directs clients to the office at the rear, where Wolf's international firm is headquartered. It accommodates up to ten employees and is outfitted with a bath and kitchenette for potential use as a future granny flat.

The floor plan's staggered levels grew out of the need to compress the building to meet the 9-meter (29.5-foot) height restriction. These level changes help define discrete spaces, which make the house more animated and, unlike rooms, can be used for different purposes, Wolf says. With strategically positioned cutaways in the inside and outside walls, "people are always seeing something different," and light from multiple windows passes through each space, eliminating the need for artificial daytime lighting.

The family spends most of its time on the ground floor's living, dining, and kitchen area, which flow out to a porch and lawn. The double-height dining room is not just for eating but serves as a place to do homework or have meetings and is a thoroughfare from one area to another. "One space flows into another; this was a way to keep the family together," Wolf says. "The vertical space was designed to feel like a cathedral, because coming together for a meal is the most sacred ritual a family performs."

Upstairs are the bedrooms and baths and a private terrace, and another staircase leads to a rooftop playroom / music studio that's also great for sunbathing and watching fireworks displays—not to mention venting hot air from the lower floors. Rainwater is collected in underground tanks and is used to irrigate the gardens, wash cars, and flush toilets.

Wolf doesn't take a conceptual or "big idea" approach to architecture, preferring instead to focus on what's practical, functional, and looks good. "This house is about responding to family and business needs and also commonsense principles" such as good light and proper solar orientation, he says. "We haven't tried to make it anything more than what it has to be."

The front porch has a sealed concrete floor that allows the children to use it as a giant blackboard. Slats on the north side shade and screen the master suite while softening the building's street facade.

❮ The key to the design is a multipurpose vertical corridor that acts as a light conduit and thermal chimney.

TW-280

"We try to design our houses so people don't have to go out and buy new furniture. Once you have to do that, you lose a lot of the soul and hominess of the home. We look for flexible, timeless pieces that could go anywhere, and don't buy new until it's busted beyond repair."

❮ "Our children sometimes like to do their homework on the stairs, which are generous and have natural light. They find it to be an interesting space, which we didn't expect."

A movable glass wall separates the house from the architecture office, which also houses one of the owner's classic cars.

TW-280

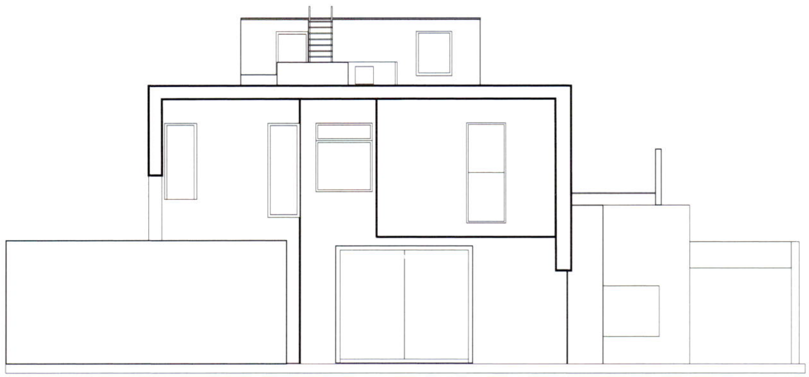

SOUTH ELEVATION

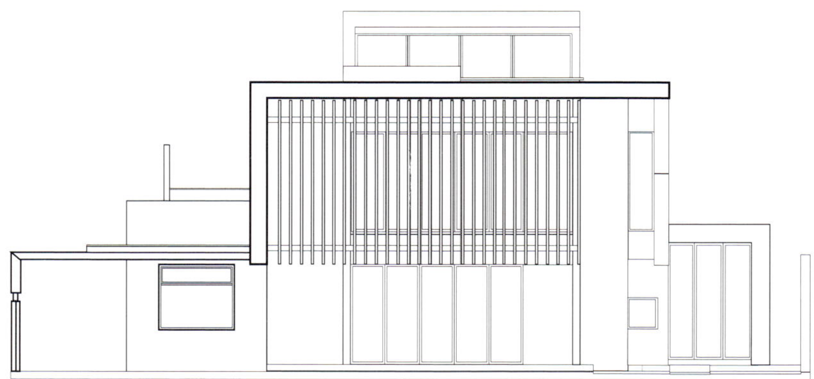

NORTH ELEVATION

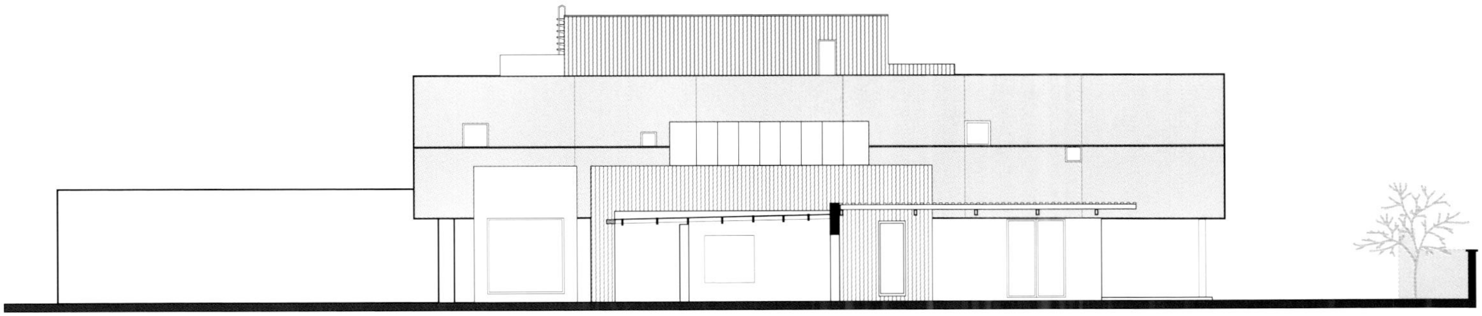

EAST ELEVATION

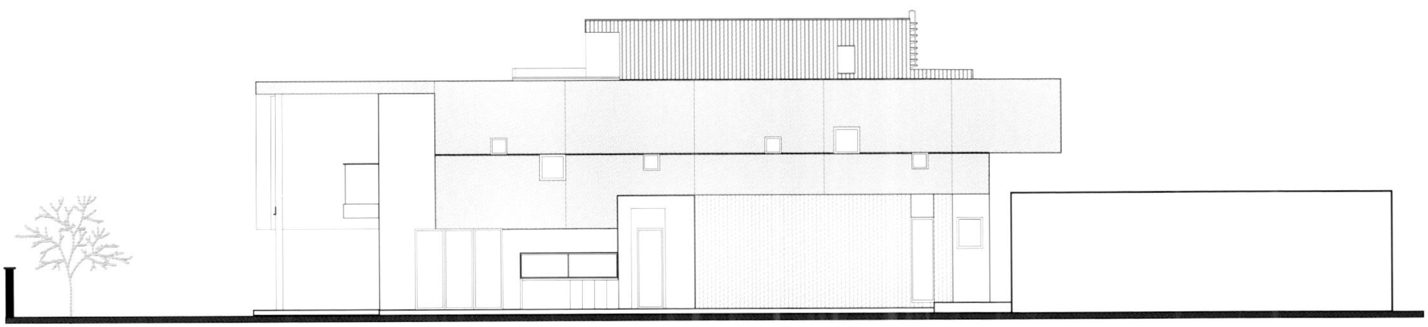

WEST ELEVATION

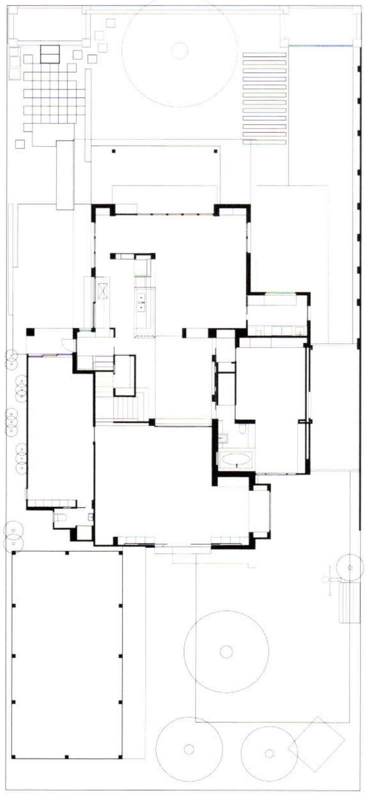

FIRST FLOOR PLAN

SECOND FLOOR PLAN

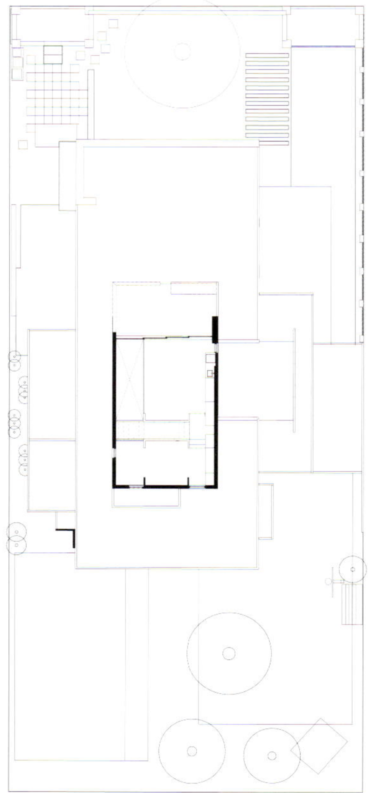

ROOF PLAN

YAMAHA

DUNALLEY HOUSE

Tasmania

15

Stuart Tanner Architects

After a bush fire burned their brick vacation home to the ground, the owners asked architect Stuart Tanner for a replacement that would be a fortress against wind, fire, and sun on this exposed site yet feel light enough to float on water. The 15-hectare (37-acre) parcel, on a headland overlooking Dunalley Bay, also prompted them to rethink the house's location. "They had always looked out to the point from their original house and said it would be nice to do something out there," Tanner says. "Standing there, you feel the vastness of the landscape, sky, and water. What could we do there? We could do anything."

In this case, "anything" turned out to be an L-shaped building that responds to the fire threat not only in the way it sits on the land, but also with its materials. Tanner drew two offset volumes bisected by a jetty-like walkway on an east–west axis. The utilitarian bedroom wing on the south sits on slightly excavated ground to protect it from wind and fire. Made of thick precast concrete, the building's south face is almost completely closed, and punched windows take in intimate views of Dunalley Bay. In contrast, the cantilevered steel-and-glass living space sits a step below the bedroom wing and is sandwiched between flying planes of roof and deck; below, the land drops off to the water. In this, Tanner was inspired by the Japanese idea that bedrooms have a higher hierarchy than social spaces. "Culturally, it's symbolic to step up to where you go to sleep," he says. "The bedroom bunker feels secure, quiet, and peaceful. Then you step down to the living space, where you are released to the view and the light."

Given the location nearly an hour from town, Tanner turned to modular building systems to reduce delivery trips. While the big, cantilevered floor slab was poured in place, the bedrooms' precast concrete and living space's semi-prefab steel frame were constructed in the city and assembled on-site. Inside the main living area, a raw timber ceiling counterpoints the industrial feel and lends a honey-colored glow.

House, climate, and culture interact both in practical and poetic ways. The northern sun tracks along the building's east–west axis, which ends at a fire pit overlooking the beach. The fire circle honors the indigenous Tasmanians, who lived around fire and took it from site to site, Tanner says. "I grew up camping in Tasmania, so it's ingrained in my psyche to sit around the campfire and stare at the stars. If my clients can do that, they start to involve themselves in the place they are."

‹ The living area's cantilevering roof tries to touch the immense landscape beyond.

An axial deck runs from the entry, through the house, to a fire pit overlooking the beach.

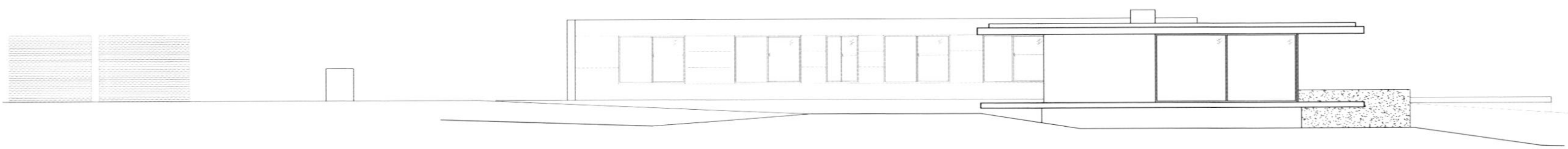

NORTH ELEVATION

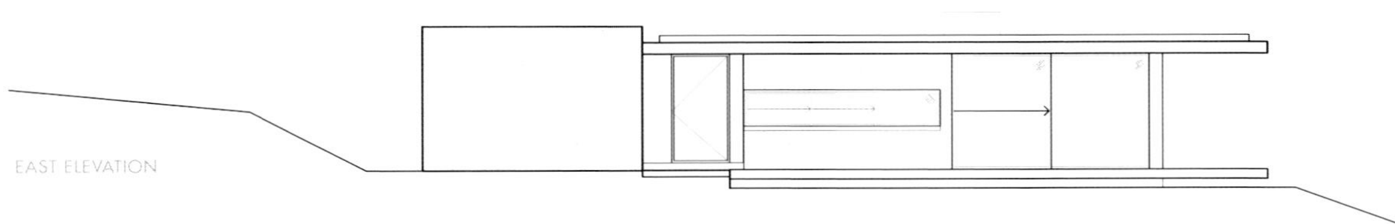

EAST ELEVATION

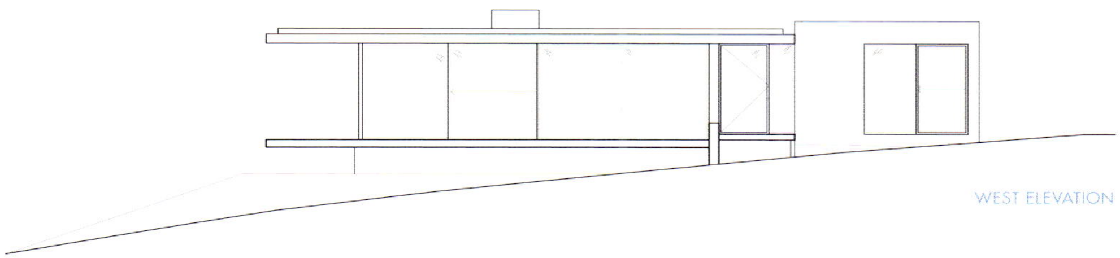

WEST ELEVATION

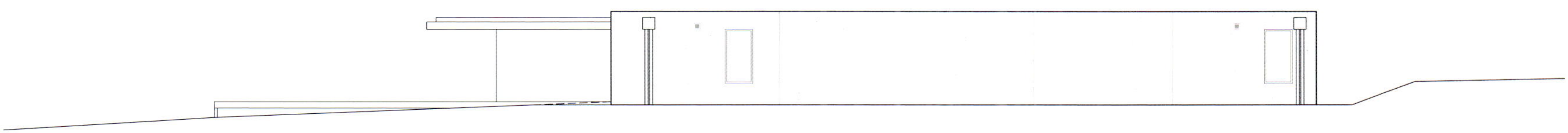

SOUTH ELEVATION

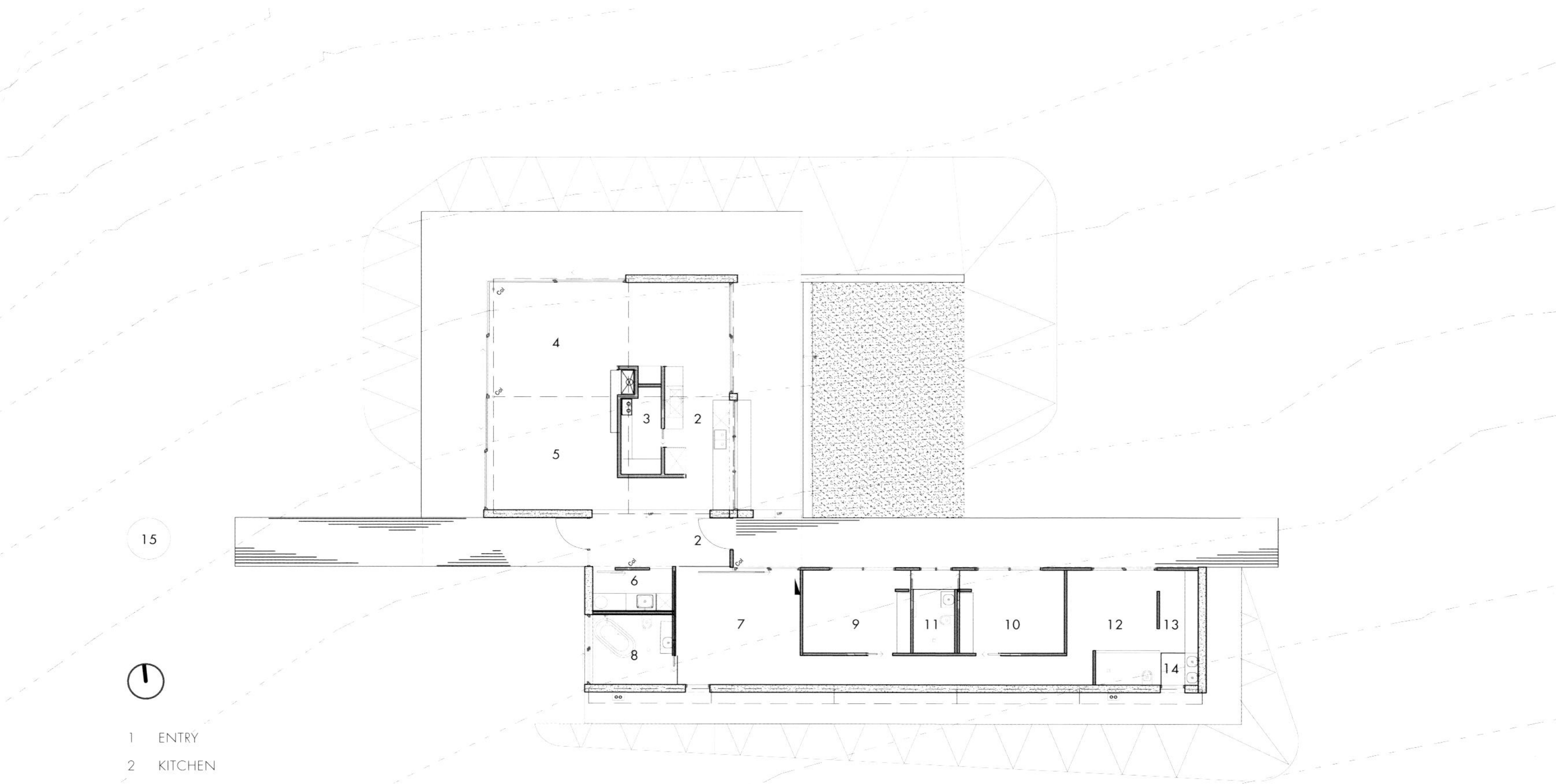

1 ENTRY
2 KITCHEN
3 PANTRY
4 DINING
5 LIVING
6 LAUNDRY
7 RUMPUS ROOM
8 BATH
9 BEDROOM 2
10 BEDROOM 3
11 SHOWER
12 MASTER BEDROOM
13 MASTER BATH
14 CLOSET
15 FIRE PIT

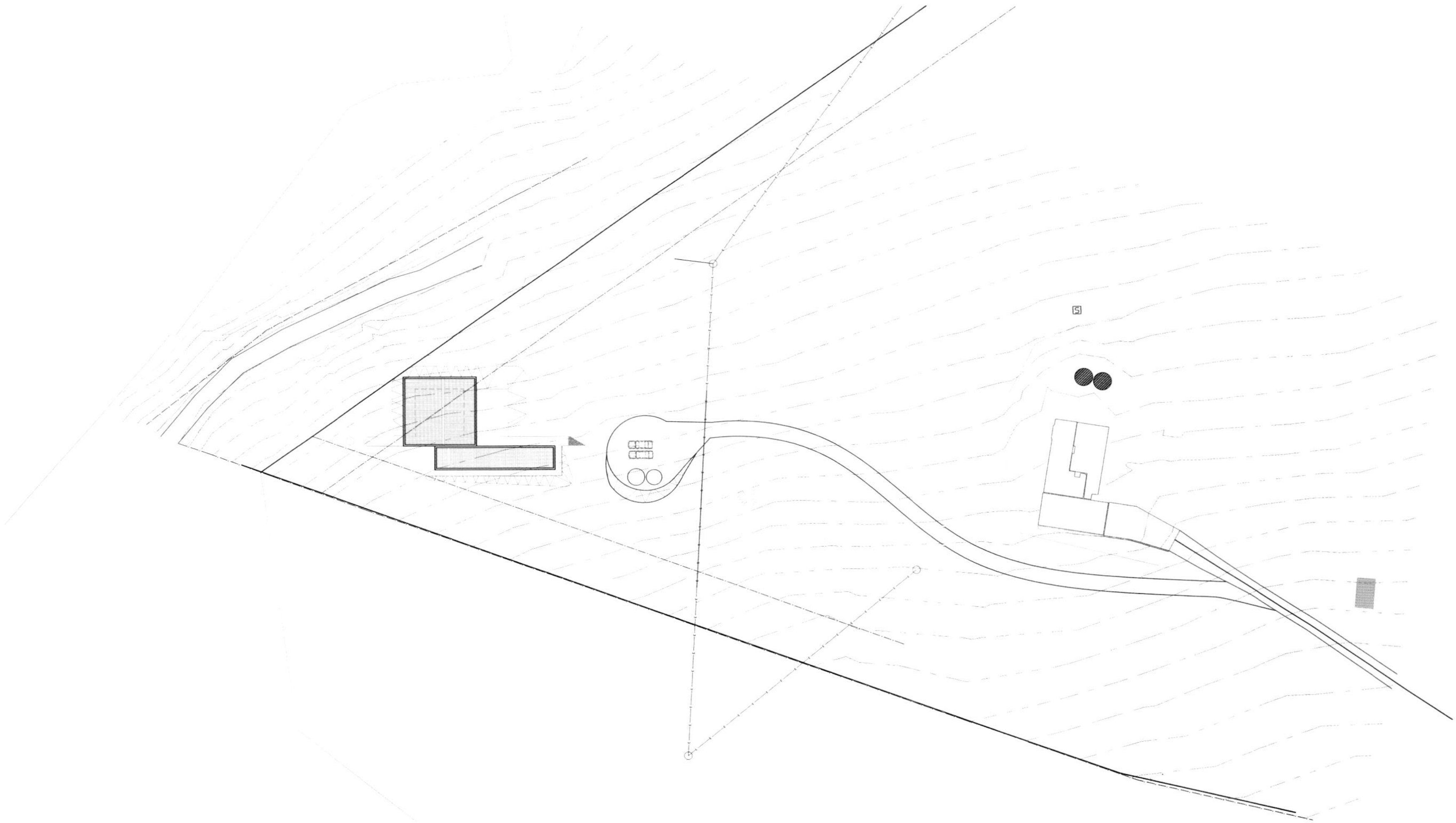

A bath in the bedroom bunker frames a view across the bay of Mount Wellington, the highest point on the horizon. The bedroom wing is made of precast concrete and sits in a depression to protect it from fire and wind.

A hovering roof shelters and shades the main living space.

Seaberg House, 2017
Kerstin Thompson Architects
www.kerstinthompson.com
Photography: Derek Swawell

Sky Barn, 2017
Max Pritchard Architect
www.maxpritchardarchitect.com.au/
Photography: Sam Noonan

Toy Management House, 2016
Austin Maynard Architects
www.maynardarchitects.com/au
Photography: Peter Bennetts

Naranga House, 2016
James Russell Architect
www.jrarch.com/au
Photography: Toby Scott

Quorrobolong House, 2014
Fergus Scott Architects
www.fergusscottarchitects.com/au
Photography: Michael Nicholson

Sunset House, 2017
Peter Stutchbury Architecture
www.peterstutchbury.com.au/
Photography: Michael Nicholson

Nikki Maloney House, 2014
Drew Heath Architects
www.drewheatharchitect.com
Photography: Brett Boardman

Charles House, 2017
Austin Maynard Architects
www.maynardarchitects.com/au
Photography: Peter Bennetts

Coogee House II, 2017
Madeleine Blanchfield Architects
www.madeleineblanchfield.com
Photography: Madeleine Blanchfield

Moonlight Cabin, 2015
Jackson Clements Burrows Architects
www.jcba.com.au/
Photography: Jeremy Weihrauch Gollings Studio

Second Valley House, 2014
Max Pritchard Architect
www.maxpritchardarchitect.com.au/
Photography: Sam Noonan

House Maher, 2013
Tribe Studio Architects
www.tribestudio.com.au/
Photography: Katherine Lu

Friedrichstrasse House, 2015
Troppo Architects
www.troppo.com.au/
Photography: vividmedia@gmail.com

Wolf House, 2015
Wolf Architects
www.wolfarchitects.com.au/
Photography: Taras Wolf

Dunalley House, 2016
Stuart Tanner Architects
www.stuarttannerarchitects.com.au/
Photography: Brett Boardman

Library of Congress Control Number: 2019935943

Written by Cheryl Weber
Project research by Steve Huyton
Designed by Danielle D. Farmer
Cover design by Brenda McCallum

Front and back covers: Sunset House designed by Peter Stutchbury Architecture, photos by Michael Nicholson
Type set in Dark Moon/Futura Std

ISBN: 978-0-7643-5812-8
Printed in China

Published by Schiffer Publishing, Ltd.
4880 Lower Valley Road
Atglen, PA 19310
Phone: (610) 593-1777;
Fax: (610) 593-2002
E-mail: Info@schifferbooks.com
Web: www.schifferbooks.com

For our complete selection of fine books on this and related subjects, please visit our website at www.schifferbooks.com. You may also write for a free catalog.

Schiffer Publishing's titles are available at special discounts for bulk purchases for sales promotions or premiums. Special editions, including personalized covers, corporate imprints, and excerpts, can be created in large quantities for special needs. For more information, contact the publisher.

We are always looking for people to write books on new and related subjects. If you have an idea for a book, please contact us at proposals@schifferbooks.com.

Other Schiffer Books by Steve Huyton:
Modern Masters, ISBN 978-0-7643-5384-0
Luxury Design for Living, ISBN 978-0-7643-5421-2

Other Schiffer Books on Related Subjects:
Anatomy of a Great Home, Boyce Thompson,
ISBN 978-0-7643-5465-6